"FOUR SCRIPT IN HAND COMEDY PLAYS"

"Bite Me"
"MacBeth The Knife"
"The Big Snooze"
"Alias Cinderella"

Written by

Bruce Kane

Copyright (c) 2025
Bruce Kane Productions

The four script in hand comedy plays in this collection are written to be performed by actors at microphones in modern dress reading from scripts.

The set may be as minimal as a row of chairs for the actors and two or three microphones for them to speak into. It can also be as elaborate as a full recreation of a recording studio or anything in between.

The cast can be a full compliment of actors or a minimal number playing all the parts and changing their vocal characteristics to represent the characters they are playing.

Because the actors will be reading from scripts rehearsal times can be reduced although performances should be honed before going on stage.

Sound effects and music can be performed live on stage or recorded and played back electronically. The latter may provide you with more variety and flexibility.

However you choose to mount your production, these are comedies. We trust you will have as much fun performing them as the audience will have in watching you.

"BITE ME"

A DICK SHAMUS MYSTERY

by Bruce Kane

"BITE ME" IS COPYRIGHTED MATERIAL AND MAY NOT BE PRODUCED OR PRESENTED IN ANY FORM WITHOUT THE EXPRESS PERMISSION OF BRUCE KANE PRODUCTIONS. TO OBTAIN A PERFORMANCE LICENSE PLEASE GO TO KANEPROD.COM/CONTACT.HTM)

(LIGHTS UP

CAST ENTERS, SCRIPTS IN HAND, AND SIT ON CHAIRS UPSTAGE. ACTORS WILL APPROACH THE MICROPHONES AT THE APPROPRIATE MOMENTS)

STAGE MANAGER
We go in five... four... three... two...

(The Stage Manager points. BLUESY FILM NOIR SAXOPHONE begins to play.)

SHAMUS
The name's Shamus. Dick Shamus. I work for the F.B.I. The Fictional Bureau of Investigation. I handle the toughest, dirtiest cases in English literature. That's right, I'm a fictional detective.

(Saxophone out. After a beat, stirring music up and under)

ANNOUNCER
It's the Adventures of Dick Shamus, Fictional Detective starring Jason Tindal as Dick Shamus, Fictional Detective. Tonight's episode "Bite Me."

(Saxophone out)

SHAMUS
Postmark Transylvania. Return address 13 Abomination Lane. Sender Abraham Van Helsing.

VAN HELSING
My dear Mr. Shamus. I'm writing to you at the suggestion of a mutual friend who wishes to remain nameless. Over the past year my country, Transylvania, has been devastated by the loss of nearly eighty per cent of our virgin population.

                          SHAMUS
What country hasn't?

                          VAN HELSING
The situation has reached crisis proportions. Our mutual
friend says you're the man to get to the bottom of this
mystery and solve our problem. Needless to say we are
desperate. Please come as soon as you can. Travel
instructions are included below. Yours truly, Dr. Abraham
Van Helsing. D.D.S., D.D.D, Ph.D. and other three letter
acronyms too numerous to mention.

                          SHAMUS
How could I refuse? I mean I wanted to refuse. Who wants to
go to Transylvania in the off season? Who wants to go to
Transylvania in any season? But, when you're a fictional
detective you go where you're needed. So, I did what I
always do when someone in trouble reaches out. I slipped on
my trench coat. Grabbed my fedora and cued my saxophone
accompaniment.

                          *(BLUESY SAXOPHONE UP AND
                          UNDER)*

                          SHAMUS
Van Helsing's directions were very clear. You leave the
Pennsylvania Station about a quarter to four.

                          (SFX: TRAIN SOUNDS)

                          SHAMUS
You read a magazine and you're in Krysetstamor. Have
breakfast in the diner. Nothing could be finer, than to
have your ham and eggs in Asia Minor.

                          (TRAIN SOUNDS OUT)

                          (SAXOPHONE OUT)

                          SHAMUS
It was midnight when the train pulled in. But this being
Transylvania, the trained always pulled in at midnight. I
made my way to The Mausoleum, a dive on the wrong side of
Cemetery Row. The right side of Cemetery Row being the
cemetery. The joint was dark, dank, dingy, damp, decaying,
decrepit, dreary, dismal and depressing. It reminded me a
dame I was once crazy about. It was "Miserable Hour" at The
Mausoleum, so naturally the place was filled with the usual
contingent of uglies, creatures, zombies, ghouls and
goblins. The Denizens greeting wasn't what you would call
warm and fuzzy.

THE DENIZENS
(spooky)
Welcome to Transylvania, where you can live your life and still be dead. Welcome to Transylvania where your days and nights are filled with dread. Welcome to Transylvania, there's no place we can think of more perverse. Welcome to Transylvania where your Uber driver shows up in a hearse.

IGOR
Well, well. If it isn't Dick Shamus, Fictional Detective.

SHAMUS
I should have known. Long time no see, Igor. Still in the monster making business.

IGOR
Gave that up a long time ago. Besides I was only a silent partner.

SHAMUS
Whatever happened to your old boss?

IGOR
Dr. Frankenstein? After the locals torched his castle, he moved to Bucharest. You could say he's brought… "new life to the town."

SHAMUS
You could say it. I never would.

IGOR
So Van Helsing took my advice.

SHAMUS
I shoulda known it was you. Your pal told me to meet him here.

IGOR
You passed him on your way in.

SHAMUS
Which one of these dead beats is he?

IGOR
You got the dead part right.

SHAMUS
What're you talkin' about?

IGOR
When I said you passed him on your way in, I was talking about the cemetery.

                              SHAMUS
What's he doin' in the cemetery?

                              IGOR
Well, he isn't taking cha cha lessons.

                              SHAMUS
You tellin' me Van Helsing is dead?

                              IGOR
If he wasn't when they buried him, he sure is now.

                              SHAMUS
What he die of?

                              IGOR
Nobody knows for sure. One day he was moving around like you
and me. Well, you anyway. The next day they were planting
him.

                              SHAMUS
Sounds a little suspicious, don't you think?

                              IGOR
This is Transylvania. Every death is suspicious.

                              SHAMUS
I was wondering if Van Helsing's death had anything to do
with the missing virgins when...

                                        *(BLUESY SAXOPHONE UP AND
                                        UNDER)*

                              SHAMUS
... she ambled in.

                              MOLLY
When hello there, tall, dark and alive. Buy a girl a drink?

                              SHAMUS
Sure thing, honey hips. What's your poison?

                              MOLLY
A Bloody Mary.

                              SHAMUS
Igor.

                              IGOR
Yes, master?

                              SHAMUS
Two Bloody Marys.

5.

IGOR
Two Bloody Marys coming up.

MOLLY
Igor is famous for his bloody marys.

SHAMUS
I'll take you word for it.

MOLLY
And what are you famous for?

SHAMUS
Not gettin' involved with dames who ask me what I'm famous for.

MOLLY
You got something against hot babes?

SHAMUS
Don't get me wrong. I like dames. Good lookin' dames. Long legged dames. Well constructed dames. And so far you're checking all the boxes. But I never get involved. In my business, getting involved could also get you dead... Permanently.

IGOR
Two Bloody Marys.

SHAMUS
She tossed her down in one gulp. I was entranced.

MOLLY
That's the best Bloody Mary I've ever had.

IGOR
That's because I make it with real blood.

MOLLY
In that case, I'll have another.

SHAMUS
A dame who could drink me under the table. It was love at first sight. From that moment on we were inseparable. Like two peas in a pod. Like cherries in a bowl. Like hot fudge and ice cream.

MOLLY
Think you can knock off the food analogies. Your making me hungry?

SHAMUS
For now.

6.

MOLLY
What say you and me flee this popsicle stand?

SHAMUS
Whatever you say, sweet knees.

MOLLY
By the way, you can call me Molly.

SHAMUS
Why's that?

MOLLY
Because it's my name.

THE DENIZENS
I decided to take Molly out for a little carriage ride in the country. Just her and me, the moonlight, a blanket and a shaker of Bloody Marys. Unfortunately the country we happened to be taking our little ride in was … Transylvania.

(SFX: THUNDER AND LIGHTNING)

MOLLY
I just love the Carpathian Mountains during the rainy season. Don't you?

SHAMUS
She was a strange girl. Incredibly well built, but strange.

MOLLY
(frightened)
Shamus...Look.

SHAMUS
What is it?

MOLLY
The bridge is out.

SHAMUS
Did you say that bridge is out?

MOLLY
That's what I said. The bridge is out.

SHAMUS
That's what I thought you said.

MOLLY
Then why did you make me repeat it.

                              SHAMUS
Dramatic emphasis.

                              MOLLY
Oh, what will we do? Just the two of us here, alone, in the
forest with only a blanket, a shaker of Bloody Marys and a
burning mutual attraction that must be satisfied before the
flames consumes us both.

                              SHAMUS
Good question. What about that joint up ahead?

                              MOLLY
You mean that dark, foreboding castle perched precipitously
over those jagged rocks being pounded by an angry and
merciless sea?

                              SHAMUS
Yeah, that castle.

                              MOLLY
It looks charming enough.

                         (SFX: FOOTSTEPS)

                              SHAMUS
Why don't you ring the bell.

                         (SFX: A WOMAN'S BLOOD CURDLING
                         SCREAM)

                              SHAMUS
Try it again.

                         (SFX: A WOMAN'S BLOOD CURDLING
                         SCREAM.)

                         (SFX: A CREAKING DOOR SLOWLY
                         OPENING)

                              RENFIELD
Yes? May I help you?
            (laughs evilly)

                              SHAMUS
The name's Shamus. Dick Shamus. The doll here calls herself
Molly.

                              RENFIELD
And why is that?

SHAMUS
It's her name. We were taking a carriage ride in the country.

RENFIELD
How romantic.

SHAMUS
Yeah. Then the storm hit and washed out the bridge.

RENFIELD
That darn bridge.
(laughs evilly)

SHAMUS
Any chance we could camp out here until the storm blows over?

RENFIELD
I'll check with the master.

MOLLY
Seems like a nice enough fellow.

SHAMUS
For a gargoyle.

MOLLY
Kind of cozy for a dark and foreboding castle perched precipitously on a precipice over an angry and merciless sea, don't you think Shamus?

SHAMUS
If your idea of a decorating choices run to early mortuary.

DRACULA
Good evening.

SHAMUS
Whoa. Where did you come from?

DRACULA
I just flew in and, boy, are my arms tired.

SHAMUS
Old joke.

DRACULA
Joke? I never joke. I have no sense of humor.

SHAMUS
Something about this guy gave me the willies. I don't know if it was the slicked back hair, the pale white complexion or the blood dripping from his fangs.

DRACULA
Allow me to introduce myself. I am... Dracula.

(OMINOUS ORGAN MUSIC STING)

DRACULA

Count Dracula.

(OMINOUS ORGAN MUSIC STING)

DRACULA
You are guests in... Dracula's Castle.

(OMINOUS MUSIC STING)

SHAMUS
Nice to meet you Count. We were just wondering if me and "tasty toes" here could camp out until the storm blows over.

DRACULA
Mi casa es su casa. The "girls" will show you to your room Mr. Shamus.

SHAMUS
Girls? What..? Before I could finish, five skinny dames in long slinky black gowns with pale, white skin and long black hair parted in the middle suddenly appeared out of nowhere. If I didn't know better I could've sworn I was at a Cher concert.

DRACULA
Allow me to introduce Mandi, Candi, Sandi, Randi and... Martha. Say hello to Mister Shamus, girls.

GIRLS
(monotonally)

Hello, Mr. Thyme.

DRACULA
If you would care to come with me Miss Molly, I'll show to a room where you can freshen up.

SHAMUS
While Molly went off with the Count, I followed Martha and the Vandellas down a dark, dank, dingy, damp, decaying, decrepit, dreary, dismal and depressing corridor. Nice place you got here, girls.

10.

> MARTHA
> (deep, monotonal,
> breathy voice,
> dripping with sexual
> innuendo)

We like it.

> SHAMUS

The girls led me to a cozy little cell furnished with a chair, a desk, a candle and a... Hey, what's with the coffin?

> MARTHA

Think of it as a... theme room.

> SHAMUS

What's the theme, a quick death?

> MARTHA

Oh no Mr. Shamus. Not quick. Not quick at all.

(SFX: DOOR CREAKING SHUT. DOOR BOLT SLAMMED SHUT)

> SHAMUS

Hey, Morticia... What's the big idea? Open up... Open up. I was locked in. Trapped like something that is trapped in something else.

(MUSICAL TRANSITION)

> DRACULA

And this is your room, my dear.

> MARTHA

Lovely. Who's your decorator, the Marquis De Sade?

> DRACULA

As a matter of fact.

> MARTHA

A ceiling mirror. Nice touch.

> DRACULA

The previous resident was an actor. Perhaps you would like to slip into something more comfortable.

> MOLLY

You mean like this bed?

> DRACULA

It does have a sleep number mattress.

MOLLY
And I can imagine the number.

DRACULA
No need to be afraid, my dear. I'm not as I'm portrayed me dear.

MOLLY
I'm not young. I'm not naive. I know exactly what's up your sleeve.

DRACULA
Just think of me like any guy whose looking for a girl whose looking for a guy like me.

MOLLY
You can save the hype, dear Count. I'm really not your type dear Count.

DRACULA
Type A or Type B, makes no difference to me.

MOLLY
No matter how you plead, dear Count. Our bodies won't be mergin'. For you see dear Count, I am still a virgin.

DRACULA
Even better... Look into my eyes, my dear.

MOLLY
Your eyes?

DRACULA
My eyes.

MOLLY
Oh Count, your eyes are quite hypnotic.

DRACULA
Tonight the die is cast, my dear.

MOLLY
This sensation's so erotic.

DRACULA
When I take you in my arms, my dear.

MOLLY
I feel so hot to trotic.

DRACULA
And bite you on the neck, my dear.

MOLLY
Oh Count...Oh Count. My next line...I forgot it.

(TRANSITIONAL MUSIC)

(CROWD NOISE OF THE MAUSOLEUM)

IGOR
Shamus... What happened to you? You look half dead. Which around here would normally be quite the complement.

SHAMUS
Dracula locked me in a cell and threw away the key. It took me three days to pick the lock. All I had to work with a shoelace, a collar button and a slow laxative.

IGOR
Where's Molly?

SHAMUS
Gone.

IGOR
Gone?

SHAMUS
Without a trace. I lost her Igor. You hear me? I lost her. I lost the only dame who... could drink me under the table.

IGOR
Girls like that are hard to find.

SHAMUS
She was one of a kind.

IGOR
What're you gonna do?

SHAMUS
I'm gonna do what any fictional detective would do when he's lost the only dame with a liver bigger than his.

IGOR
What's that?

SHAMUS
What else? I'm gonna get stinkin' drunk. Bring on those Bloody Marys.

(MUSICAL TRANSITION)

                    SHAMUS
              (drunk as a skunk)
Hey, what are you lookin' at you bag of bones? Yeah, I'm
talking to you mister ugly.

                    IGOR
Hey, Shamus. There's no need to be mean cause we all look
like Halloween. We may not be attractive. And some are radio
active. But, if a kindness you will show us and really get to
know us, think about the friends we all could be.

                    SHAMUS
              (belligerent)
Friends? With this bunch of rag and bones?

                    IGOR
We feel we have to warn you, that we would truly mourn you,
if you call us all a horrible disgrace.

                    SHAMUS
Oh yeah? What are you gonna do about it?

                    IGOR
There's only one thing we can do. And here is just a little
clue.

                    SHAMUS
              (still belligerent
               and drunk)
Clue? What clue?

                    DENIZENS
We will have to eat your face.

                    SHAMUS
You and what army?

                         (SFX: SHAMUS BEING PUMMELED BY
                         THE DENIZENS)

                         (TRANSITIONAL MUSIC)

                    NURSE CLAVICLE
Now, now Mr. Thyme. You sustained quite a beating. You know
the doctor said you shouldn't get excited.

                    SHAMUS
Then he shouldn't have made you my nurse.

                    NURSE CLAVICLE
That's enough of that. I'll be right back with your
medicine.

14.

> **SHAMUS**
> You better be talkin' a fifth of scotch. Nurse Clavicle was takin' pretty good care of me. But, something was nagging at me. It was the little voice in the back of my head.

> **LITTLE VOICE**
> What're you doin' Shamus? Laying around here watchin' reruns of Oprah. You're a dick, and don't you forget it.

> **SHAMUS**
> That's fictional dick to you.

> **LITTLE VOICE**
> You make me sick. You make me ill. You're not the only one around here needs a pill. There's a dame out there who could be dead or even worse and what are you doin? Playin' footsie with your nurse.

> **SHAMUS**
> Did I mention it was an annoying little voice?

> **LITTLE VOICE**
> You make me sick. I feel unwell. To think that dame could be wrapped up in Dracula's spell. Forget the pain. Forget the hurt. Get outta bed. Go find that skirt.

> **SHAMUS**
> The little voice was right. What am I doing laying around here feeling sorry myself? Molly needs me.

> **LITTLE VOICE**
> Now, that's the Dick Shamus in whose head I live, unfortunately.

> **SHAMUS**
> I'll follow every clue. I'll track down every lead. There's nothing I won't do until that girl is freed. I'm Dick Shamus, the world's greatest fictional detective.

> **LITTLE VOICE**
> No to mention the world's only fictional detective.

> **NURSE CLAVICLE**
> Mr. Shamus, you shouldn't be out of bed.

> **SHAMUS**
> I've got a job to do apple knees and I can't do it lyin' around here. There's a dame out there that needs my help. She's sweet, she's innocent and she's built like a brick pagoda.

> **NURSE CLAVICLE**
> Oh, that's so romantic.

15.

SHAMUS
Do me a favor, cantaloupe lips. Calls this number. Tell the dame on the other end to dig up everything she can on a mug name Dracula.

(OMINOUS ORGAN MUSIC STING)

SHAMUS
Count Dracula.

(OMINOUS ORGAN MUSIC STING)

SHAMUS
Last known address, 21 Bloodsucker Terrace, Transylvania. Got that?

NURSE CLAVICLE
Got it.

SHAMUS
And while you're at it, give her your phone number.

NURSE CLAVICLE
My phone number?

SHAMUS
Just in case things don't work out with the brick pagoda.

(TRANSITIONAL MUSIC)

SHAMUS
Effie, my sweet, did you track down the info on that Dracula character I asked for.

EFFIE
Sure, thing boss.

SHAMUS
What'd you find?

EFFIE
From what I could acquire, he's no member of the choir. Just you average, everyday, blood sucking vampire. His need for blood is dire. Constant victims he requires. Prefers his victims sweet and young, before their virtue's been undone. To fulfill his lustful urges, he's in constant search of virgins.

SHAMUS
Now it all makes sense.

                              EFFIE
A bullet cannot kill him. A knife's a big mistake. The only
thing that seems to work is a hammer and a wooden stake.

                              SHAMUS
Good work, cumquat hips.

                              EFFIE
If you need me for anything else, just buzz. You know how to
buzz, don'tcha boss? You just put your lips together and...

                        (SFX: BUZZING SOUND)

                              SHAMUS
I watched Effie pulsate out of my office, put my eyes back
on either side of my nose and went to work trying to figure
out where I could find Dracula.

                        (OMINOUS MUSIC STING)

                          LITTLE VOICE
Here we go again. Why couldn't I have been the little voice
in George Clooney's head. Come on Shamus. This is a no
brainer which puts it right in your sweet spot. All you have
to do is put yourself in Dracula's place.

                              SHAMUS
Maybe if I put myself in Dracula's place. Okay, I've put
myself in Dracula's place.

                          LITTLE VOICE
Ask yourself this. If I was Dracula, where would I go?

                              SHAMUS
If I was Dracula, where would I go?

                          LITTLE VOICE
Well?

                              SHAMUS
Where would I go? Of course. Albuquerque!

                          LITTLE VOICE
That's just plain jerky.

                              SHAMUS
How about Katmandu?

                          LITTLE VOICE
How about Katmandon't?

                              SHAMUS
Budapest?

LITTLE VOICE
Give it a rest. Let's try another tack. If I was Dracula ...
I'd go someplace familiar.

SHAMUS
Someplace familiar. Someplace familiar.

LITTLE VOICE
Like someplace there is no place like.

SHAMUS
Someplace there is no place like. Now, what is someplace there is no place like?

LITTLE VOICE
How about blank sweet blank? Forget it. Let's just cut to the chase. How about Dracula is going home!

SHAMUS
I can almost touch it.

LITTLE VOICE
How about... DRACULA... IS... GOING... HOME!!!!

SHAMUS
It's on the tip of my tongue. I can practically taste it.

LITTLE VOICE
How about? Dracula is going home to Transylvania you thick headed yutz.

SHAMUS
I've got it.

LITTLE VOICE
Got what?

SHAMUS
Dracula is going home to Transylvania, you thick headed yutz.

(TRANSITIONAL MUSIC)

(SFX: LOW CROWD CONVERSATION)

SHAMUS
I decided to drop in at The Mausoleum, for old time's sake. Nothing had changed. And, everything reminded me of her. Even the cigarette butts in the ashtray were round and firm and fully packed.

                    IGOR
It's been a long time, Shamus. Never thought you'd show your
face in here again.

                    SHAMUS
Igor looked the same. Butt ugly.

                    IGOR
You ain't exactly Tom Selleck. What're you drinkin'?

                    SHAMUS
Make it a decaf vanilla latte. Heavy on the decaf.

                    IGOR
You're puttin' me on.

                    SHAMUS
I'm off the sauce, Igor.

                    IGOR
Lemme guess, a dame.

                    SHAMUS
Didn't know it showed.

                    IGOR
Dames, there's nothing like 'em

                    SHAMUS
Nothing in this world.

                    IGOR
There is nothing you can name.

                    SHAMUS
That is anything like a dame.

                    LITTLE VOICE
Hey, Shamus. Knock off the lyricizing. You're embarrassing
yourself not to mention setting yourself up for some hefty
royalty payments.

                    IGOR
One decaf vanilla latte.

                    VAMPIRE MOLLY
Well, hello there tall, dark and decaffienated.

                    SHAMUS
Suddenly she was there on the stool next to me. She was
wearing a long, black slinky dress. Her skin was pale and
white. Her hair was long and black and parted down the
middle.

                    VAMPIRE MOLLY
Buy a girl a drink?

                    SHAMUS
Sure. Igor.

                    VAMPIRE MOLLY
A Bloody Mary. Make it with Type O.

                    IGOR
I'll open a vein.

                    VAMPIRE MOLLY
Remember me?

                    SHAMUS
Mandi?

                    VAMPIRE MOLLY
Try again.

                    SHAMUS
Randi?

                    VAMPIRE MOLLY
Not even close.

                    SHAMUS
Candi?

                    VAMPIRE MOLLY
Uh uh.

                    SHAMUS
Sandi.

                    VAMPIRE MOLLY
Sorry.

                    SHAMUS
Don't tell me your Martha.

                    VAMPIRE MOLLY
Okay I won't.

                    SHAMUS
Who are you then?

                    VAMPIRE MOLLY
You can call me Molly.

                    SHAMUS
Why should I?

VAMPIRE MOLLY
Cause it's my name.

SHAMUS
It couldn't be. Nothing about her was the same.

VAMPIRE MOLLY
I heard you were back.

SHAMUS
News travels fast.

VAMPIRE MOLLY
Transylvania is a small town. What're you doing here Shamus?

SHAMUS
I came to take you back.

VAMPIRE MOLLY
Forget me Shamus.

SHAMUS
I'm not leaving without you.

VAMPIRE MOLLY
The sun will be coming up soon. I have to go.

SHAMUS
What did he do? What did he put in his elixir. You're not the girl I once knew, when you were the hottest shiksa.

VAMPIRE MOLLY
He cast his spell, then rang my bell. He took control and then my soul. But all in all, my life's quite swell. I'm free of pain. I'm free of dread. I have no fear of growing old. I never count cholesterol.

SHAMUS
I never knew a dame like you. That winning smile. I want it back. And don't forget that world class rack.

VAMPIRE MOLLY
Don't waste your time with one more rhyme. My days with you were never pallid. But tell me Shamus, what's in your wallet? The truth is there in black and white. Once you go Drac, you never go back.

SHAMUS
And with that she was gone. Gone with the wind.

IGOR
Another latte, Shamus?

                    SHAMUS
Gimme a Bloody Mary, Igor. And this time make it O negative.

                    IGOR
The hard stuff. You sure, Shamus?

                    SHAMUS
Of all the mausoleums in all the towns in all of
Transylvania, she had to walk into this one. Do me a favor,
Igor. Play it.

                    IGOR
Play it?

                    SHAMUS
You know what I want to hear. If she can stand it, so can I.
Play it Igor.

                         *(MUSIC: THE BACH CONTATA ON
                         ORGAN. MUSIC FADES.)*

                    SHAMUS
For Transylvania, the weather was unseasonably mild.

                         (SFX: THUNDER AND LIGHTNING)

                    SHAMUS
I found my way back to Dracula's Castle and rang the bell.

                         *(SFX: WOMAN'S BLOOD CURDLING
                         SCREAM)*

                    SHAMUS
I tried the door. It was locked. I found a window, pushed it
open and climbed in. The room was filled with coffins as far
as the eye could see. It looked like the showroom at Forest
Lawn. The lid to an elaborately carved casket slowly rose
up. There he was, Count Dracula, dressed immaculately in a
perfectly tailored Pierre Cardin tuxedo with matching red
lined cape. You had to hand it to the guy. He really knew
how to accessorize.

                    DRACULA
Good evening, Mr. Shamus. I wasn't expecting you.

                    SHAMUS
I've come for the girl.

                    DRACULA
I'm afraid you'll have to be more specific. My castle is
filled with ghouls.

SHAMUS
Not a ghoul. A girl.

DRACULA
And which girl would that be.

SHAMUS
Let's just call her Molly.

DRACULA
And why is that?

SHAMUS
It's her name. I decided I needed a little persuasion so I pulled out my gat. Hand her over.

DRACULA
Unless you're the Lone Ranger and that gun has silver bullets, I'm afraid it will do you no good. You see I'm already dead.

SHAMUS
How about this?

DRACULA
A wooden stake. Now that would do it.

SHAMUS
I'm going to drive this stake right through your heart, bat boy. At last, all those hours of watching "The Old House" were going to pay off.

VAMPIRE MOLLY
No, no Shamus. I won't let you kill him.

SHAMUS
Get out of the way corpse girl.

VAMPIRE MOLLY
I love him, I love him and where he goes I'll follow.

SHAMUS
Knock off the Motown and step away from the vampire.

DRACULA
Renfield!

SHAMUS
You called master?

DRACULA
Renfield, how would you like to have an assistant?

RENFIELD

An assistant master?

DRACULA

Yes. You're own assistant. Someone to do whatever you tell him to do.

RENFIELD

Like sweeping up the bat guano.

DRACULA

Yes, Renfield, like sweeping up the bat guano.

RENFIELD

I would like that very much, master.

DRACULA

Good. You can start by grasping Mr. Shamus's arms and pinning them behind his back.

SHAMUS

Hey, let go. Let go I tell you. For a dead guy Renfield had a helluva grip.

DRACULA

You've become an annoyance, Mr. Shamus. It's time for you to go.

SHAMUS

You forget one thing, Count.

DRACULA

And what would that be, Mr. Shamus?

SHAMUS

That.

DRACULA
(panicking)

Sunlight. It can't be. It's too early.

SHAMUS

You forgot one thing, Drac. Daylight savings time. Fall back. Spring forward.

DRACULA
(voice weakening)

Damn you Renfield. Why didn't you warn me? What do I pay you for?

RENFIELD
(voice weakening)

You don't, you cheap...

DRACULA
In that case, remind me to defund your retirement plan.

SHAMUS
It's lights out for you Count. I'm going to nail you to that wall.

DRACULA
One request, Mr. Shamus, Mr. Shamus before you drive that stake through my heart.

SHAMUS
What's that?

DRACULA
Don't drive that stake through my heart.

SHAMUS
Request denied.

(SFX: HAMMER HITTING WOODEN STAKE)

VAN HELSING
You did it Mr. Shamus. You've saved Tranyslvania.

SHAMUS
Who the hell are you?

VAN HELSING
I'm Abraham Van Helsing.

SHAMUS
I thought you were dead.

VAN HELSING
I was.

SHAMUS
I don't get it.

VAN HELSING
While I was one of the living dead, you knew me as Renfield.

SHAMUS
Renfield? You?

VAN HELSING
But now that Dracula is no longer, I have returned to once again being the the handsome and debonair Doctor Alexander Van Helsing, the man other men want to be and women want to be with and sometimes vice versa. But we won't go into that here.

MOLLY
Shamus... Shamus.

SHAMUS
Molly is that you?

MOLLY
Yes, it's me. I'm free, I'm alive and I'm still a virgin.

SHAMUS
Well, two outta three ain't bad.

(STIRRING MUSIC UP AND UNDER)

ANNOUNCER
You've been listening to "The Adventures of Dick Shamus, Fictional Detective." Join us next week for another exciting case from the files of Dick Shamus, Fictional Detective. This is your announcer speaking.

<u>THE END</u>

"MACBETH THE KNIFE

A DICK SHAMUS MYSTERY

by Bruce Kane

("MACBETH THE KNIFE" IS COPYRIGHTED MATERIAL AND MAY NOT BE PRODUCED OR PRESENTED IN ANY FORM WITHOUT THE EXPRESS PERMISSION OF BRUCE KANE PRODUCTIONS. TO OBTAIN A PERFORMANCE LICENSE PLEASE GO TO KANEPROD.COM/CONTACT.HTM)

(The cast, scripts in hand, file in and take seats behind stand up microphones. The Actors approach the microphones when appropriate)

STAGE MANAGER
We go in five... four... three... two...

(The Stage Manager points. BLUESY FILM NOIR SAXOPHONE is heard.)

SHAMUS
The name's Shamus. Dick Shamus. I work for the F.B.I. The Fictional Bureau of Investigation. I handle the toughest, dirtiest cases in English literature. That's right, I'm a fictional detective.

(Saxophone out. After a beat, stirring music up and under)

ANNOUNCER
It's the Adventures of Dick Shamus, Fictional Detective starring Jason Tindal as Dick Shamus, Fictional Detective. Tonight's episode "MacBeth The Knife."

(Music out)

SHAMUS
It was raining that Monday I got back to the office. I'd just spent six weeks at sea on a tub called The Pequod. The captain had taken up permanent residence in Davey Jones Locker and I was there to find out why. Was it murder? Was it an accident? Everyone I talked to told me the same thing, almost like it had been written out for them. The captain was killed by a whale. Not just any whale. A white whale. It had to be true. Who would ever come up with a story like that? I was writing up my report when Effluenza Wachowski, my over developed secretary with the under developed typing skills, pulsated into my office in four inch stiletto heels.

(SFX: Drumbeats emphasize Effie's walk)

EFFIE
Three inch stilettos are for nuns.

SHAMUS
She told me I had a visitor.

EFFIE
You got a visitor.

SHAMUS
I told her to tell him I'm busy. Tell him I'm busy. She said he'd come a long way to see me.

EFFIE
He's come a long way to see you.

SHAMUS
I asked her how far is long? How far is long? She said Scotland.

EFFIE
Scotland.

SHAMUS
That is long. I asked her what he wanted. What does he want? She said..

EFFIE
How long are you gonna keep doing that?

SHAMUS
Sorry, apple hips, just establishing a style. Anything else I should know?

EFFIE
He has a very unusual fashion sense.

SHAMUS
Meaning?

EFFIE
Meaning, he's wearing a plaid mini skirt.

SHAMUS
Really?

EFFIE
Really.

SHAMUS
You've peaked my curiosity, tangerine cheeks. Have the gentleman come right in.

EFFIE
(bellowing)
Come on in!!!

(Door opens)

MALCOLM
(Scotch accent)
Mr. Shamus?

SHAMUS
I'm Shamus.

MALCOLM
Me name is Malcolm.

SHAMUS
Please, to meet you Malcolm. Have a seat.

MALCOLM
Thank you.

SHAMUS
He sat down, modestly crossed his legs at the ankles and straightened his hem.

EFFIE
If you want me for anything else boss, just whistle. You know how to whistle, don'tcha? You just put your lips together and...

SHAMUS
And what?

EFFIE
Do I have to think of everything?

(SFX: Door closes.)

SHAMUS
What can I do for you, Malcolm?

MALCOLM
I need your help.

SHAMUS
That's what I'm here for.

30.

>   MALCOLM
> I want you to catch a murderer.
>
>   SHAMUS
> Murder, huh? Interesting. Who got whacked?
>
>   MALCOLM
> Me father.
>
>   SHAMUS
> I'm sorry to hear that. What makes you think your old man
> was murdered?
>
>   MALCOLM
> The seven stab wounds in his back.
>
>   SHAMUS
> I immediately ruled out suicide. Malcolm said that back home
> his father had been a big deal.
>
>   MALCOLM
> Back home me father was a big deal.
>
>   SHAMUS
> How big?
>
>   MALCOLM
> The biggest. He was king.
>
>   SHAMUS
> It don't get much bigger than that. Any idea who did it?
>
>   MALCOLM
> One.
>
>   SHAMUS
> Does he have a name?
>
>   MALCOLM
> Everyone has a name.
>
>   SHAMUS
> I know that. I was just setting up a dramatic reveal.
>
>   MALCOLM
> Oh. In that case his name is...
>   (dramatically)
> MacBeth.
>
>   *(Dramatic music sting)*

                              SHAMUS
The King of Scotland had gotten his ticket punched and it
was up to me to find out who his travel agent was. Your case
intrigues me Malcolm. I'll take it.

                              MALCOLM
Thank you, Mr. Shamus.

                              SHAMUS
I think we should split up. Travel separately.

                              MALCOLM
I'll take the high road.

                              SHAMUS
I'll take the low road.

                              MALCOLM
I'll get to Scotland afore yee.

                    *(SFX: Thunder, wind howling,
                    rain falling)*

                              SHAMUS
Cold, wet and miserable I stumbled into "The Inn Of The
Three Witches." Ramshackle, tumble down, off the beaten path
in a secluded part of a remote forest it wasn't exactly a
Starbucks. But, then again, there wasn't one on every
corner. I was shaking off the rain when a snaggled tooth
crone with rotting flesh dropped into the chair next to me.

                              HECATE
Well, 'ello there tall, dark and miserable. What'll it be?

                              SHAMUS
Whaddya got?

                              HECATE
We got a nice fenny snake.

                              SHAMUS
How do you cook that?

                              HECATE
In the cauldron boil and bake.

                              SHAMUS
Anything else?

                              HECATE
There's eye of newt, toe of frog, wool of bat, tongue of
dog, Adder's fork, blind worm's sting and the 'ouse
                              (MORE)

HECATE (cont'd)
special... lizard's leg. We serve that with a mixed green salad, of course.

SHAMUS
Of course.

HECATE
As for the more discerning palate, there's nose of Turk and Tartar's lips.

SHAMUS
For some reason my appetite took a powder. I'll just settle for directions, sweet knees.

HECATE
Suit yourself. But, you're passin' up a real mouth watering treat, y'are.

SHAMUS
I'm looking for Dunsinane Castle.

HECATE
Goin' to see the MacBeth's are ya?

SHAMUS
Just the directions, toots.

HECATE
He was here himself, he was. Macbeth. Sat right where you're sittin'. Old high and mighty. Course, we knew he was comin' so we put on our best rags, we did. Gave 'im a real show, we did. 'Ad the fire burnin' and the cauldron bubblin'. We was a sight alright. Prophysyin'... Tellin' 'im 'ow he was gonna be the big cheese and all. 'E loved, 'e did. You shoulda seem him. Rode outta here all puffed up like Christmas goose, 'e was.

SHAMUS
About those directions.

HECATE
Sure you don't wanna 'ang around till closin'? I get off at midnight, if you know what I mean.

SHAMUS
I knew exactly what she meant. That's why I was out the door faster than you can say acid reflux.

(SFX: Thunder, wind howling)

SHAMUS
Cold, wet and miserable I stumbled out of the darkness and into Dunsinane Castle.

GUARD

Who goes there?

SHAMUS

The name's Shamus... Dick Shamus. I'm here to see the king. Official business.

GUARD

Wait here.

(Musical interlude to indicate passage of time)

GUARD

Okay, Shamus. You're cleared. Follow me.

(SFX: During the following we hear footsteps, doors opening, doors closing, more footsteps, more doors opening and closing.)

SHAMUS

The guard led me through a small ante room, just off a waiting room, next to a dining room, behind a reception room, that opened onto a sitting room, that overlooked a garden room, that led to a stairway, around a tower, through an armory, around a kitchen, into another ante-room that led into the throne room. Excuse me.

GUARD

Yes?

SHAMUS

Isn't there a shortcut or something?

GUARD

This is the shortcut.

(Door opens)

SHAMUS

When we finally got where ever it was we were going...

GUARD

Mr. Shamus, ma'am.

(MUSIC: Bluesy film noir saxophone)

SHAMUS

She was there. Waiting for me.

                          LADY MACBETH
                          (sultry voice)
I've been waiting for you.

                             SHAMUS
Nola? Nola MacDougal?

                          LADY MACBETH
Funny, no one's called me that in ages.

                             SHAMUS
Back when I knew her, everyone called her Nola. She was a
showgirl with orange feathers in her hair and a dress cut
down to there. In those days Nola was beautiful, smart,
ambitious, dangerous, scheming, conniving, calculating and
cunning. In short, she was everything I ever wanted in a
woman.

                        (Saxophone out)

                             SHAMUS
The years had been kind to Nola, although, I had to admit,
she'd changed. You haven't changed a bit Nola. If anything,
she'd added a few more erogenous zones. Mmmmmm, I liked that
line. I decided to go with it. If anything, tangerine toes,
you've added a few more erogenous zones.

                          LADY MACBETH
You always did know the right thing to say to a girl, didn't
you Shamus?

                             SHAMUS
It worked. I'd have to remember it.

                          LADY MACBETH
Still mad at me, Shamus?

                             SHAMUS
Why? Because you dumped me without saying a word?

                          LADY MACBETH
Maybe.

                             SHAMUS
Because you slipped out of my life one night and disappeared
without so much as a post-it note?

                          LADY MACBETH
Perhaps.

                             SHAMUS
Because you ripped out my heart and stomped on it with those
three inch sling back, open toed, stiletto heels you always
                             (MORE)

SHAMUS (cont'd)
wore with black seamed stockings and a red dress the showed off more curves than Sandy Koufax the day he struck out eighteen.

LADY MACBETH
I'm glad to see you're a man who doesn't hold a grudge.

SHAMUS
Just one question.

LADY MACBETH
Sure.

SHAMUS
Why? Give me one good reason.

LADY MACBETH
He could offer me wealth. He could offer me power. He could offer me...

SHAMUS
I said just one.

LADY MACBETH
What could you offer me, Shamus? A fictional detective's pay? An underfunded retirement account? Admit it Shamus, I had no future with you. . I was just someone to feed your insatiable passion. Bank the fires of your raging lust. Satisfy your...

SHAMUS
She was killing me softly with her words. I had to shut her up and I knew just how to do it.

LADY MACBETH
Shamus... Shamus...
(swooning)
Ohhhh, Shamus.

(Musical transition)

LADY MACBETH
(sighing)
I can't remember the last time two minutes flew by so quickly. So, tell me Shamus... what are you doing here? And don't tell me you came all this way just for a little highland "fling."

SHAMUS
I'm investigating a death.

LADY MACBETH
Who died?

                        SHAMUS
The King.

                        LADY MACBETH
The King? Don't be ridiculous. The king is in perfect
health.

                        SHAMUS
How come you know so much about the King of Scotland?

                        LADY MACBETH
Well... for one thing, my name's not Nola MacDougal anymore.
It's...

                        SHAMUS
Yes?

                        LADY MACBETH
MacBeth.

                        (Dramatic music sting)

                        LADY MACBETH
Lady MacBeth.

                        (Dramatic music sting)

                        SHAMUS
That means the king is...

                        LADY MACBETH
My husband.

                        SHAMUS
Did you say husband?

                        LADY MACBETH
Yeah... That's what I said. Husband.

                        SHAMUS
That's what I thought you said.

                        LADY MACBETH
Then why did you make me repeat it?

                        SHAMUS
Dramatic effect. Husband. That word had a way of focusing a
man's attention. I hadn't even started my investigation and
the case had already gotten complicated. According to the
code of the fictional detective you don't fool around with
the wife of your prime suspect. Of course, I didn't know she
was the wife of my prime suspect at the time I took her on a
trip to ecstacyville. So technicality wise, I was off the
                        (MORE)

                    SHAMUS (cont'd)
hook. Somehow, I couldn't picture Nola mixed up in murder.
Extortion, blackmail, bookmaking, mail fraud... sure. But
murder? Like I said, it was getting complicated.

                    LADY MACBETH
Are you done?

                    SHAMUS
For now. Nola told me I was wasting my time.

                    LADY MACBETH
Your wasting your time.

                    SHAMUS
She said they found the men who murdered King Duncan.

                    LADY MACBETH
We found the men who murdered King Duncan.

                    SHAMUS
She said their hands were drenched in blood.

                    LADY MACBETH
Their hands were drenched in blood.

                    SHAMUS
She said...

                    LADY MACBETH
Could you please stop doing that.

                    SHAMUS
I'd like to talk to them, these killers of yours.

                    LADY MACBETH
Too late.

                    SHAMUS
How so?

                    LADY MACBETH
You know those gargoyles hanging on the front gate when you
came in?

                    SHAMUS
Yeah.

                    LADY MACBETH
Those aren't gargoyles.

                    SHAMUS
Why the rush to judgment?

> **LADY MACBETH**
> To assure the peasants that justice had been served. That society was back in balance one again. That they could return to their miserable lives and that we could return to making them miserable.

> **SHAMUS**
> Not that I don't believe every word you're telling me, cumquat ears. Yeah... Right... Nola couldn't draw a straight line with a ruler. If it's okay I'll just hang around and ask a few questions, just for appearances sake.

> **LADY MACBETH**
> You do that, Shamus.

> **SHAMUS**
> Just for the record, where were you when the king got whacked?

> **LADY MACBETH**
> In my room. And, I've got seven witnesses to prove it.

> **SHAMUS**
> Knowing Nola, I was surprised it was only seven. One more thing, persimmon hips... When you talk to your husband...

> **LADY MACBETH**
> Yes?

> **SHAMUS**
> I wouldn't say anything about what went down here. I wouldn't want him to get the right idea.

> **LADY MACBETH**
> No problem. I've forgotten it already.

(Musical transition)

> **SHAMUS**
> Before I could figure out whodunit, I first had to figure out whocouldadunit. My modus operandi - that's Latin for modus operandi. And you thought I was just another pretty face. Like I said, my modus operandi is to ask a lot of questions. Sometimes you get answers and sometimes you don't get answers and sometimes the answers you don't get are more important than the answers you do get. The only problem you didn't get 'em.

> **SHAMUS**
> Excuse me, sir.

MACDUFF
Yes, what is it?

SHAMUS
Mind if I ask you a lot of questions?

MACDUFF
Depends on who's doing the asking.

SHAMUS
The name's Shamus.

MACDUFF
The fictional detective

SHAMUS
Word travels fast.

MACDUFF
Lady MacBeth said you'd be nosin' around.

SHAMUS
What else did she say?

MACDUFF
That you were a complete stranger. That she'd never seen you before and that I shouldn't listen to ugly rumors.

SHAMUS
Just for the record, what's your name?

MACDUFF
MacDuff.

SHAMUS
You work for MacBeth, MacGruff?

MACDUFF
MacDuff. It's MacDuff.

SHAMUS
MacDuff.

MACDUFF
I work for MacBeth. You might say I'm his right hand man.

SHAMUS
And who would you say is his left hand man?

MACDUFF
I didn't know he had a left hand.

                              SHAMUS
Everybody's got a left hand.

                              MACDUFF
If you say so.

                              SHAMUS
You wouldn't happen to know where MacBeth was when King
Duncan got dead.

                              MACDUFF
You don't think MacBeth had anything to do with the king's
death.

                              SHAMUS
Just asking.

                              MACDUFF
You're barking up the wrong tree, mister. MacBeth had no
reason to kill Duncan.

                              SHAMUS
What makes you think that? He got to be king didn't he?

                              MACDUFF
MacBeth never wanted to be king. He was perfectly happy
being Thane of Cawdor. Stealing from the peasants.
Oppressing the serfs. Sleeping with the scullery maids. Then
the witches told him he'd be Thane of Glammis.

                              SHAMUS
Thane of Glammis?

                              MACDUFF
It's the castle on the Frammis.

                              SHAMUS
MacBeth is thane of Glammis on the Frammis?.

                              MACDUFF
No. Like I told you. MacBeth is Thane of Cawdor.

                              SHAMUS
Then who's Thane of Glammis on the Frammis?

                              MACDUFF
Tammis.

                              SHAMUS
Tammis?

                              MACDUFF
Yes. Tammis of Glammis on the Frammis.

                          SHAMUS
It all sounded like double talk to me. Tell me something
MacGruff...

                          MACDUFF
MacDuff. It's MacDuff.

                          SHAMUS
MacDuff. How did MacBeth react to Duncan's kickin' the
bucket?

                          MACDUFF
He was really broken up by it. He loved Duncan like a
father. He hasn't been the same fun lovin', peasant taxing,
wife stealing guy he used to be.

                          SHAMUS
How is he different?

                          MACDUFF
Spends most every day and night wandering the halls, talking
to himself.

                          MACBETH
                       (reciting)
I am always chasing rainbows.

                          MACDUFF
Like that.

                          SHAMUS
Suddenly, there he was. Big Mac himself.

                          MACBETH
Watching clouds drifting by.

                          MACDUFF
If you've got nothing else, Shamus, I'm out of here.

                          SHAMUS
For some reason the sudden appearance of the king had
spooked MacGruff.

                          MACDUFF
                    (from a distance)
MacDuff. It's MacDuff.

                          MACBETH
My schemes are like all my dreams. Ending in the...

                          SHAMUS
Your majesty.

MACBETH
Is this a dagger I see before me? The handle toward my heart.

SHAMUS
No. Actually, it's a soup spoon.

MACBETH
Damn, I coulda sworn it was a dagger.

SHAMUS
No, it's a soup spoon,

MACBETH
Are you sure?

SHAMUS
Positive.

MACBETH
Good thing I didn't try to stab anybody with it. How embarrassing would that be?

SHAMUS
Your highness, could I ask you a few questions?

MACBETH
How many is a few?

SHAMUS
More than some. Less than a bunch.

MACBETH
That sounds good. By the way, who are you?

SHAMUS
The name's Shamus.

MACBETH
The fictional detective. My wife mentioned you.

SHAMUS
Really? And what did she say, if I may ask?

MACBETH
That you were a complete stranger. That she'd never seen you before and that I shouldn't listen to ugly rumors. What is it you wanted to know?

SHAMUS
Just curious as to where you were when King Duncan bought the farm?

                        MACBETH
Bought the farm? You must have me confused with Old
McDonald.

                        SHAMUS
No. Where were you when King Duncan was iced? Whacked?
Shivved?

                        MACBETH
I don't understand.

                        SHAMUS
Murdered?

                        MACBETH
That I understand. I was in my quarters. And I've got seven
witnesses to prove it.

                        SHAMUS
So far everybody had an alibi. It was the same alibi, but it
was an alibi.

                        MACBETH
                (voice trailing off)
Some fellows look and find the sunshine. I always look and
find the rain.

                    (SFX: Thunder, wind, rain)

                        SHAMUS
Something MacGruff said...

                        MACDUFF
                (from a distance)
MacDuff. It's MacDuff.

                        SHAMUS
Something MacDuff said kept rattling around in my brain like
a loose screw. I decided to check it out.

                    (End of sound effects.)

                        SHAMUS
Wet, cold and miserable, I stumbled back into The Inn Of The
Three Witches.

                        HECATE
Well, look who's 'ere. Couldn't say away from ole Hecate,
could ya, duckie?

                        SHAMUS
What can I say liver face? You're sore eyes are a sight.

HECATE
'Ow you do go on.

SHAMUS
The last time I was here, you told me MacBeth had been sitting where I was sitting.

HECATE
Same exact spot.

SHAMUS
That you gave him a real show.

HECATE
That we did.

SHAMUS
You also said you knew he was coming.

HECATE
That's right.

SHAMUS
How did you know he was coming?

HECATE
She told us.

SHAMUS
She? Who?

HECATE
Never told us her name. Just handed me a pouch full of gold coins, she did.

SHAMUS
What did she look like?

HECATE
About so high. Wore a red dress, she did. With them stockings with the seams up the back and them shoes with real high pointy heels.

SHAMUS
Stilettos.

HECATE
'Ad one of them, too.

SHAMUS
Why did she want you to know MacBeth was coming here?

HECATE
Said it was his birthday. Wanted us to give him a special show. Even wrote it all out for us. Told her we'd be real 'appy to do it, but there was one teensy, weensy, little problem.

SHAMUS
What was that?

HECATE
None of us can read.

SHAMUS
What did she do?

HECATE
Got right up on that table and did the whole number for us, she did. Ain't never seen nothin' like it.

SHAMUS
That had to be Nola. She always did her best work on a table top. Could you show me what she had you do?

HECATE
Sure.
            (calls out)
Latasha... Latoya... Lashana.

SHAMUS
Three of the most decrepit crones to ever haunt a stage shuffled out and hit it.

THE THREE WITCHES
            (sing)
All hail MacBeth, new thane of Glammis
Thou shalt be king and that's a promise
Be strong, be proud and take no sass
Ain't no here can kick your ass.
MacBeth shall never vanquished be,
Until Birnham Wood come to Dunsinane see.
That's your future short and tall.
And now we're outta here, y'all.

(Musical transition)

SHAMUS
It was all starting to make sense. But proving it wasn't going to be easy. It never is.

(SFX: Thunder, wind, rain)

SHAMUS
Wet, cold and miserable, I stumbled back into the castle.
The place was quiet... Dead quiet.

(SFX. Very loud bonging of a clock.)

SHAMUS
Except for that. I opened the door to the cell that was
passing for my room when I saw it. A knife stuck in the
mattress where my back would have been. That knife raised a
lot of questions. Who was trying to kill me? Why did MacBeth
walk around reciting pop tunes? And why did King Duncan's
son wear a skirt? If I wanted to stay alive, I had to be
careful moving around the castle. Someone had put a bullseye
on my back. I pulled the knife out of the mattress and
backed out of the room. I was cautiously making my way along
a narrow corridor when a door opened and a man stepped out.
I couldn't tell who it was but I recognized the woman posed
seductively in the doorway.

LADY MACBETH
I can't remember the last time two minutes went by so...
quickly.

SHAMUS
I couldn't understand his reply. It's hard to hear what a
guy is saying when he's got a tongue in his mouth...that
isn't his own. I waited for the dame to close the door then
moved in.

SHAMUS
MacGruff.

MACDUFF
It's MacDuff. MacDuff.

SHAMUS
Surprised?

MACDUFF
Surprised? No. Why should I be surprised?

SHAMUS
I don't know. You look surprised. You sound surprised. You
act surprised.

MACDUFF
I'm surprised you'd think I was surprised.

SHAMUS
Then you're not surprised?

47.

MACDUFF
No, of course I'm not surprised.

SHAMUS
I find that surprising.

MACDUFF
I'm surprised that you're surprised that I'm not surprised.

SHAMUS
Considering I just caught you playing tonsil hockey with the lady of the house.

MACDUFF
It's not what it seems.

SHAMUS
It isn't?

MACDUFF
Okay, it is what it seems. You're not gonna tell the king are you?

SHAMUS
What you and the first lady do is your own business.

MACDUFF
Thanks, Shamus. I owe you one.

SHAMUS
It's time to pay up.

MACDUFF
So soon? Isn't there usually a gap, a grace period?

SHAMUS
Do you know where Lady MacBeth was when King Duncan turned up face down.

MACDUFF
Lady MacBeth had nothin' do with the Duncan's death. You do anything to upset the lady and you'll have me to answer to. You got that Shamus?

SHAMUS
You like Lady MacBeth, don't you?

MACDUFF
Yeah... Sure... What's not to like? She's kind, gentle, sweet and loving. You don't know here like I do Shamus.
(suspiciously)
You don't know her like I do, do ya Shamus?

                         SHAMUS
Apparently not. You'd do anything for Lady MacBeth wouldn't
you?

                         MACDUFF
You bet your bodkin I would.

                         SHAMUS
Like kill for her?

                         MACDUFF
Only if she asked me... Hey, what are you getting at?

                         SHAMUS
One more question. Where were you when Duncan got whacked?

                         MACDUFF
With Lady MacBeth. And we've gotten seven witnesses to prove
it.

                         SHAMUS
MacGruff's alibi..

                         MACDUFF
That's MacDuff. MacDuff.

                         SHAMUS
MacDuff's alibi got me to wondering what they were doing
that required seven witnesses. I was about to ask him when...

                         MACBETH
                      (reciting)
Day and night. Night and day.

                         MACDUFF
It's the king.

                         MACBETH
Why is it so that this longing for you follows where ever I
go?

                         MACDUFF
If he asks, I was never here and I've got seven witnesses to
prove it.

                         SHAMUS
Your majesty.

                         MACBETH
                   (a little tipsy)
Shamus... Is that you?

SHAMUS
It's me.

MACBETH
Wanna a little drinkie?

SHAMUS
Some other time.

MACBETH
You don't know what you're missing... Hundred year old scotch... Imported.

SHAMUS
You know anything about this?

MACBETH
Is that a soup spoon I see before me?

SHAMUS
It's a knife. Recognize it?

MACBETH
It's mine.

SHAMUS
So you admit it.

MACBETH
Admit what?

SHAMUS
That you tried to kill me.

MACBETH
I didn't try to kill you.

SHAMUS
You didn't?

MACBETH
No. I killed you.

SHAMUS
I was standing there right in front of him and he was talking like I was a dead man. Just for conversation sake, can I ask why you killed me?

MACBETH
She told me too.

SHAMUS
She told you to?

                                    MACBETH
The one and only Lady MacBeth. Sure you don't want a little
drinkie?

                                    SHAMUS
No thanks. Did she tell you why she wanted me dead?

                                    MACBETH
I don't know. Why does any woman want any man dead?

                                    SHAMUS
Good point. Did she give you a specific reason?

                                    MACBETH
She did say you were a good detective. That sooner or later
you'd figure out I'd killed Duncan.

                                    SHAMUS
Did she tell you to do that too? Kill Duncan.

                                    MACBETH
You don't know my wife like I do, Shamus.
                                (suspiciously)
You don't know my wife like I do, do you Shamus?

                                    SHAMUS
No, no. Of course I don't. The guy tried to kill me once
already, I didn't see any reason to make him mad.

                                    MACBETH
She wanted to be Queen. I mean, what woman doesn't want to
be a queen? It is a step up from princess. And in order to
become a queen in Scotland, a woman has to be married to a
king. That's the rule. I didn't make the rule. Somebody
else made the rule. But that's the rule. And a rule is rule.
And only a ruler can change the rule. That's another rule.

                                    SHAMUS
I get it. I get it.

                                    MACBETH
I wasn't a king, back then. I was a thane. I liked being a
thane. It's a good job being a thane. You get to hunt when
you want. Fish when you want. Play a little golf when you
want. You play golf, Mr. Shamus?

                                    SHAMUS
A little.

                                    MACBETH
The Scotch invented golf. Did you know that?

                                51.

                          SHAMUS
No, I didn't.

                          MACBETH
It's true. We invented golf. Golf and haggis.

                          SHAMUS
Great. Two things that give you indigestion. Why are you
telling me all this?

                          MACBETH
Why not? You're a ghost. Who are you going to tell?

                          SHAMUS
So, that's it. MacBeth thinks I'm a ghost. Either he was
drunker than I thought or mad as a hatter. But, then again,
this was twelfth century Scotland. These guys believed in
wood sprites.

                          MACBETH
Besides, what difference does it make who I tell? I'm
invincible.

                          SHAMUS
Nobody's invincible.

                          MACBETH
I am. The prophecy says so. I will reign as king until
Birnham Wood comes to Dunsinane. And there are only two
chances of that happening. Slim and...Well, one other I
can't think of right off. Sure you don't want a little
drink?

                          SHAMUS
I had my confession. But there wasn't anything I could do
with it. The king had me in check. It was time to bring
Malcolm up to date.

                    (SFX: Thunder, rain, wind)

                          SHAMUS
Wet, cold and miserable,I stumbled into Malcolm's camp.

                          GUARD
Who goes there?

                          SHAMUS
Dick Shamus, fictional detective. I'm here to see Malcolm,
son of Duncan, brother of Donalden, cousin of Sean, uncle of
Hamish and close personal friend of Phil.

                          GUARD
Aye, we've been waitin' for ya'. I'll take you to Malcolm.

SHAMUS
The guard led me across a stream, around a meadow, down a path, through a wood, along a creek, over a hill, down a dale and up to the heather on the hill.

SHAMUS
Isn't there a shorter way?

GUARD
This is the shorter way.

MALCOLM
Greetings Dick Shamus.

SHAMUS
Greetings, Malcolm.

MALCOLM
What news do you have for us?

SHAMUS
I've got good news and bad news.

MALCOLM
Me and my men could use some good news.

SHAMUS
The good news is you're in the clear. MacBeth copped to everything. Killing your father... Stealing the crown.

MALCOLM
Aye, that is good news. We must to action. My men are going crazy sitting around all day listening to bagpipe music.

SHAMUS
I don't blame them.

MALCOLM
We'll attack Dunsinane Castle in the morrow and I will claim my rightful crown.

SHAMUS
That's the bad news. There's no way three hundred men in skirts are going to take Dunsinane Castle.

MALCOLM
If me and my laddies have to spend one more day here in Birnham Wood, we'll...

SHAMUS
Wait a minute. Did you say Birnham Wood?

53.

MALCOLM
Aye. That's what I said. This is Birnham Wood.

SHAMUS
That's what I thought you said.

MALCOLM
Then why did you make me repeat it?

SHAMUS
Dramatic effect. Malcolm, I think I know a way to make this work.

MALCOLM
Let's hear it man.

(Musical interlude to indicate passage of time)

SHAMUS
Then you storm the castle, capture MacBeth and snatch the crown.

MALCOLM
Shamus, I do believe your plan is just crazy enough to work.

(SFX: Thunder, wind, rain)

SHAMUS
Cold, wet and miserable, I slipped back into the castle. It was quiet...Dead quiet.

(SFX: Loud gong striking several times)

SHAMUS
Except for that. I made my way quietly down the corridor and slipped into my room.

LADY MACBETH
Hello, Shamus.

(Saxophone plays)

SHAMUS
She was waiting for me.

LADY MACBETH
I was waiting for you.

SHAMUS
I asked what I could for her. What can I do for you? She said...

54.

> **LADY MACBETH**
> We're not going to go through that again, are we?

> **SHAMUS**
> No, not if you don't want to.

> **LADY MACBETH**
> There's something you should know.

> **SHAMUS**
> What's that?

> **LADY MACBETH**
> MacBeth confessed.

> **SHAMUS**
> I know. I was there.

> **LADY MACBETH**
> No. I don't mean you. I mean he confessed to me that he confessed to you.

> **SHAMUS**
> MacBeth confessed to you that he confessed to me.

> **LADY MACBETH**
> Yes, he confessed to me that he confessed to you.

> **SHAMUS**
> I have to confess, I'm surprised that he confessed to you that he confessed to me,

> **LADY MACBETH**
> I'm surprised he confessed to you.

> **SHAMUS**
> Why do you think he did it? Confess to you that he confessed to me.

> **LADY MACBETH**
> Because he was never cut out to be king. He can't handle the pressure. When push came to shove he wasn't capable of screwing his courage to the sticking place.

> **SHAMUS**
> Screw what?

> **LADY MACBETH**
> His courage to the sticking place?

> **SHAMUS**
> What the hell is the sticking place?

LADY MACBETH
It's the place you stick things.

SHAMUS
Well, if you stick things to it, then why would you screw something to it?

LADY MACBETH
Beats the hell out of me. MacBeth is not like you, Shamus. We used to be a great team, remember?

SHAMUS
What are you suggesting, cinammon ears?

LADY MACBETH
Why don't you come over here and we can "discuss" it.

SHAMUS
Nola had something up her sleeve. Or she would have, if she'd had a sleeve. The code of the fictional detective clearly states you never take an accessory to murder on a trip to the moon on gossamer wings. However, addendum 5, paragraph 7, subparagraph 8, states that it is not only permissible but encouraged if it's in pursuit of evidence and the party in question is put together like a brick pagoda. I made a mental note to send a case of Chateau Lafayette-we-are-here to the guy who wrote that addendum.

LADY MACBETH
Shamus, how would like to be King of Scotland?

SHAMUS
I don't know. I never thought about it. What does it pay?

LADY MACBETH
If you're interested, I think I can swing it.

SHAMUS
Isn't there already a king?

LADY MACBETH
There's going to be an opening very shortly.

SHAMUS
Can I give you my answer in the morning?

LADY MACBETH
Sure... There's no rush.

(Musical transition)

                    LADY MACBETH
When I said there was no rush, Shamus, I meant there was no
rush.

                              *(SFX: Shouts, running
                              footsteps, muffled commands)*

                    LADY MACBETH
What's going on out there?

                    SHAMUS
Stay here, vanilla knees. I'll see what's happening.

                              *(SFX: Door opens, sounds grow
                              louder)*

                    SHAMUS
MacGruff...What's going on?

                    MACDUFF
That's MacDuff... MacDuff

                    SHAMUS
Whatever. Why are all these knights, bishops and pawns
running around?

                    MACDUFF
The castle is under attack.

                    LADY MACBETH
Attack? Who's attacking the castle?

                    MACDUFF
I's Malcolm, his army and three annoying bagpipers.

                    LADY MACBETH
Where's the king?

                    MACDUFF
On the battlements.

                    LADY MACBETH
Fending off the attackers?

                    MACDUFF
Reciting iambic pentameter.

                    LADY MACBETH
We'd better get up there.

                    MACDUFF
No, please don't go, milady. It's too dangerous. Stay here
with me. I'll protect you.

LADY MACBETH
You're kidding, right?

MACDUFF
This is our chance, highness. While the battle goes on out front, we can slip out the back. Just you and me.

LADY MACBETH
Really? Just you and me. Out the back?

MACDUFF
I own some land on the bonnie, bonnie banks of Loch Lomond. We could build a cottage. Raise sheep.

LADY MACBETH
Of course. You and me. Just what I've always wanted to do, raise sheep. But first you must do something for me.

MACDUFF
Anything for you, milady.

LADY MACBETH
I want you to go up on the battlements...

MACDUFF
Yes, milady.

LADY MACBETH
And I want you to do what you do best.

MACDUFF
Of course, milady. Do what I do best.

LADY MACBETH
That's right.

MACDUFF
One question, milady.

LADY MACBETH
Yes?

MACDUFF
What is it I do best?

LADY MACBETH
Why, making yourself a target, of course.

MACDUFF
Of course, your majesty.
(calling out)
Fear not, MacBeth, I am coming.

LADY MACBETH
Oh what fools these mortals be. Especially the male mortals. This is the chance we've been waiting for, Shamus. Follow me.

SHAMUS
Where are we going?

LADY MACBETH
Up that stairway to the corridor that runs through the upper tower, around the armory, down the ladder, across the bridge, down the stairs, over the ramp, up the stairs that lead to the lower tower through the door and across the battlements.

SHAMUS
Isn't there a shortcut?

LADY MACBETH
That is the shortcut.

(SFX: Footsteps, doors opening, doors closing, more footsteps, chains rattling, gates squeaking. This give ways to the noise of battle... Trumpets, men shouting.)

LADY MACBETH
We're here.

SHAMUS
Ever think of putting in an elevator?

MACBETH
(sounding very Shakespearean)
If it were done when tis done, then 'twere well it were done quickly.

LADY MACBETH
He's right, Shamus. Let's do it. Right here. Right now.

SHAMUS
As much as I'd love to, I don't think we've got two minutes to spare. In case you haven't noticed, the castle is under attack.

LADY MACBETH
Don't flatter yourself, flatfoot. This our chance to make MacBeth mac dead.

                              SHAMUS
I've got a better idea.

                           LADY MACBETH
What's that?

                              SHAMUS
He thinks I'm dead, right?

                           LADY MACBETH
Right.

                              SHAMUS
Let's go with that.
                    (sounding ghostly)
MacBeth... MacBeth...

                             MACBETH
Who calls my name?

                              SHAMUS
It is I. The ghost of Dick Shamus.

                             MACBETH
Begone, ghost of Dick Shamus. Begone.

                              SHAMUS
Fat chance. The jig is up. You're through.

                             MACBETH
The jig will be up when Birnham Wood comes to Dunsinane.

                              SHAMUS
Look around you MacBeth. What do you see?

                             MACBETH
Trees... As far as the eye can see... Nothing but trees.

                              SHAMUS
Yes, trees. But you're missing the big picture. You're not
seeing the forest for the trees.

                             MACBETH
Ah yes, I see it now. A forest. A big green, advancing
forest.

                              SHAMUS
Do you recognize the forest?

                             MACBETH
Yes. It's... It's... Ohhhhh sh...

60.

                         SHAMUS
That's right MacBeth. Birnham Wood has come to Dunsinane.

                         MACBETH
But how is that possible?

                         SHAMUS
Malcolm relocated Birnham Wood to Dunsinane.

                         MACBETH
Every branch? Every leaf?

                         SHAMUS
Every twig. Like I always say, you can't make an omelete
without causing an ecological disaster.

                         MACBETH
I must flee. A horse... A horse... My kingdom for a horse.

                         LADY MACBETH
Wrong play you Scottish has been. It's all over... You're
through... Turn in your crown and clean out your desk.

                         MACBETH
I don't understand. What's happening?

                         LADY MACBETH
Call it a hostile takeover.

                         MACBETH
The prophecy has come to pass.

                         LADY MACBETH
There was no prophecy, you moron. I paid off the witches to
tell you all that garbage so you'd have the cojones to knock
off Duncan and I could become Queen.

                         MACBETH
There is no prophecy?

                         LADY MACBETH
Just like Shamus here isn't a ghost.

                         MACBETH
Of course he's a ghost. I killed him

                         SHAMUS
                    (normal voice)
Sorry to bust your bubble, Mac. But all you killed was my
mattress.

MACBETH

Listen to me haggis for brains. There's no such thing as ghosts. There's no such thing as witches. There's no such thing as prophecies and the tooth fairy doesn't leave money under your pillow.

MACBETH

Then who does?

MALCOLM

It worked laddie.

SHAMUS

Malcolm

MALCOLM

Your plan worked. We've captured Dunsinane.

SHAMUS

They're all yours Malcolm.

LADY MACBETH

What are you talking about Shamus? We had a deal, remember? You would get rid of MacBeth, marry me and together we would rule this land. And, in the tradition of those kings and queens before us, we'd suck the peasants dry.

SHAMUS

You had a deal, Nola. But you forget one thing.

LADY MACBETH

What's that?

SHAMUS

I'm a cop, a gumshoe, a dick.

LADY MACBETH

You can say that again.

SHAMUS

Sometimes it's good business to let people think you're corrupt. They trust you more.

MACDUFF

Milady... Milady...

LADY MACBETH

What is it MacGruff?

MACDUFF

MacDuff... MacDuff.

                              LADY MACBETH
Whatever.

                                MACDUFF
What's to become of me? I did everything you asked.

                                SHAMUS
What do you mean everything she asked?

                              LADY MACBETH
Don't say a word.

                                SHAMUS
Come on, kid... Spill. She can't do anything to you now.
What did you mean "everything?"

                                MACDUFF
Like for instance, doin' away with those two poor
unfortunates.

                                SHAMUS
Which two unfortunates.

                                MACDUFF
Those two poor unfortunates starin' down at ya from the
front gate.

                                SHAMUS
That was you?

                                MACDUFF
She made me do it, Shamus. I didn't wanna do it. She made me
kill 'em. And, all the time she knew it. I guess she always
knew it.

                                SHAMUS
Poor kid. He never had a chance. Better men than him have
gotten caught in Nola's web. He made the mistake of falling
for a dame who promised him a trip to the moon on gossamer
wings, and instead booked him a coach seat to hell. Come to
think of, every coach seat is hell.

                                MALCOLM
I'll take that crown now MacBeth. Life, as you knew it, is
over.

                                MACBETH
                          (sound very
                           Shakesperean)
Life... What is life? Life's but a walking shadow, a poor
player that struts and frets his hour upon the stage and
then is heard no more. It is a tale told by an idiot, full
of sound and fury, signifying nothing.

63.

LADY MACBETH
Spare me, the rhyming couplets.

SHAMUS
She's all your Malcolm.

LADY MACBETH
How can you do this, Shamus? Don't I mean anything to you. What about the times I fed your insatiable passion? Banked the fires of your raging lust? Satisfied your...

MACBETH
You fed his insatiable passion? Banked the fires of his raging lust?

SHAMUS
Like there was no tomorrow.

MACBETH
You never banked my fires.

LADY MACBETH
Because you're a sniveling coward. Not like Malcolm here. Now this is a real man.

MALCOLM
You really think so?

LADY MACBETH
(seductively)
Oh yes, I do. Are you not a man who stands up for what he believes?

MALCOLM
You could say that.

LADY MACBETH
I just did. Are you not a man willing to fight and die for his country?

MALCOLM
That is true. Very true.

LADY MACBETH
And are you not a man who does it all in a flattering, knee length tartan plaid skirt by Stella McCartney?

SHAMUS
It was over. King Duncan's killers had been exposed. Malcolm had been exonerated and returned to his rightful place on the throne. Now it was his turn to bleed the peasants dry.

MACBETH
Out, out brief candle.

SHAMUS
As for MacBeth... Well, in the end he was just an ordinary guy who wanted what ordinary guys want. To hunt a little. Fish a little. Get in a round of golf and now and then... Sleep with the help. Of all the characters I've come across, MacBeth has to be the most tragic.

MACBETH
Tomorrow and tomorrow and tomorrow
Creeps in this petty pace from day to day
To the last syllable of recorded time
And all our yesterdays have lighted fools
The way to dusty death.

SHAMUS
Not to mention the most depressing. And, finally there was Nola.

LADY MACBETH
Oh, Malcolm, a king like you needs a queen by his side who'll feed his insatiable passion? Bank his fires.

MALCOLM
My fires do need banking from time to time.

LADY MACBETH
And no one banks a fire likes yours truly.

SHAMUS
Like the man said...Whatever Nola wants, Nola gets.

*(SFX: Thunder, wind, rain.
Saxophone music up and out.)*

ANNOUNCER
You've been listening to "The Adventures Of Dick Shamus, Fictional Detective." Turn in next week for another episode from the files of "Dick Shamus, Fictional Detective." This is your announcer speaking.

<u>THE END</u>

"THE BIG SNOOZE"

A DICK SHAMUS MYSTERY

by Bruce Kane

"The Big Snooze" is copyrighted material and may not be produced or presented in any form without the written consent of Bruce Kane Productions. To request a royalty free license, please go to kaneprod.com/contact.htm

STAGE MANAGER
We go in five... four... three... two...

(The Stage Manager points. Bluesy film noir saxophone is heard. After a moment, the actor playing Shamus speaks)

SHAMUS
The name's Shamus. Dick Shamus. I work for the F.B.I. The Fictional Bureau of Investigation. I handle the toughest, dirtiest cases in English literature. That's right, I'm a fictional detective.

(Saxophone out. After a beat, stirring music up and under)

ANNOUNCER
It's the Adventures of Dick Shamus, Fictional Detective starring Jason Tindal as Dick Shamus, Fictional Detective. Tonight's episode "The Big Snooze."

(BLUESY FILM NOIR SAXOPHONE)

SHAMUS
It all began once upon a time when Effie, my long suffering secretary, told me I'd had a call.

EFFIE
You had a call.

SHAMUS
Who from?

EFFIE
Some guy named Dumpty.

SHAMUS
Williams Jefferson Dumpty?

EFFIE
Know him?

SHAMUS
Yeah, I know him. He helped me out on a case a few years back.

EFFIE
Now he says he needs your help.

SHAMUS
Say what about?

EFFIE
Said he couldn't talk about it over the phone.

SHAMUS
How'd he sound?

EFFIE
Scared. Said for you to grab the next boat to Peppermint Bay.

SHAMUS
Did you say Peppermint Bay?

(DRAMATIC MUSIC STING)

EFFIE
Yeah. That's what I said. Peppermint Bay.

(DRAMATIC MUSIC STING)

SHAMUS
That's what I thought you said.

EFFIE
Then why did you make me repeat it?

SHAMUS
Dramatic emphasis.

(DRAMATIC MUSIC STING)

EFFIE
Say, boss. Peppermint Bay? Isn't that the place where bon bons play on the sunny beach?

SHAMUS
Don't let the brochures fool ya. Take away the cotton candy, the gingerbread houses, the little furry woodland creatures singing pop tunes in high, squeaky voices and Peppermint Bay is just like any other burg. Corrupt... Depraved... Debauched. In short, it's my kind of town. Dumpty say where I could find him?

                              EFFIE
Said he'd be sittin' on the dock of the bay.

                              SHAMUS
Say what he'd be doin'?

                              EFFIE
Watchin' the tide roll away.

                              SHAMUS
Effie, my sweet, book me a one way ticket on the Good Ship
Lollipop. Destination Peppermint Bay.

                         (TRANSITIONAL MUSIC)

                              SHAMUS
Way back when Dumpty helped me out, I told him I owed him a
favor. Of course, I never expected him take me up on it.
Leave it to Dumpty not to recognize an empty gesture when he
heard one. It was no wonder nobody liked him. So here I was
in Peppermint Bay looking for one William Jefferson Dumpty.
When I finally found him, he wasn't exactly sittin' on the
dock of the bay. More like he was all over it.

                            (CROWD NOISE)

                            MACDOUGALL
                         (Irish accent)
Move it along... Move it along... This is an accident scene, not
a pop up book.

                              SHAMUS
Lemme guess. Dumpty.

                            MACDOUGALL
That's right laddie. Humpty Dumpty.

                              SHAMUS
He hated that name. His mother hung it on him when he was a
kid. She thought it was funny.

                            MACDOUGALL
And you wonder why some people turn out the way they do.

                              SHAMUS
How'd he buy it?

                            MACDOUGALL
Sat on that wall. Had a great fall.

                              SHAMUS
Tough way to go.

MACDOUGALL
We did everything we could for him, but it was no use.

SHAMUS
What about all the king's horses and all the king's men?

MACDOUGALL
Budget cuts.

SHAMUS
When did it happen?

MACDOUGALL
One o'clock.

SHAMUS
Who found him?

MACDOUGALL
Hickory Dickory Dock

SHAMUS
Who's Hickory Dickery Dock?

MACDOUGALL
A mouse.

SHAMUS
A mouse?

MACDOUGALL
That's right. A mouse. Runs up and down the clock.

SHAMUS
Why?

MACDOUGALL
He's a mouse. What else is he gonna do? Dumpty a friend of yours.

SHAMUS
You could say that.

MACDOUGALL
I just did.

SHAMUS
Dumpty helped me out on a case sometimes back.

MACDOUGALL
You a cop or something?

SHAMUS
The name's Shamus.

MACDOUGALL
Shamus?

SHAMUS
Dick Shamus. I work for the F.B.I?

MACDOUGALL
The F.B.I?

SHAMUS
The Fictional Bureau of Investigation. I handle the toughest, dirtiest cases in English literature.

MACDOUGALL
Then, that would make you...

SHAMUS
That's right. I'm a fictional detective.

MACDOUGALL
The name's MacDougal.

SHAMUS
The local constable, right?

MACDOUGALL
What gave me away?

SHAMUS
For one thing, the Keystone Kop outfit.

MACDOUGALL
Think this was an accident?

SHAMUS
Maybe.

MACDOUGALL
Think he was pushed?

SHAMUS
Could be.

MACDOUGALL
Think you can figure it out?

SHAMUS
Possibly.

MACDOUGALL

It won't be easy.

SHAMUS

Maybe I'll win or maybe I'll lose. Or maybe I'll end up singing the blues. But nevertheless…

MACDOUGALL

Yeah?

SHAMUS

I'd like to look around. See what I can see and what I can't see. Sometimes what you can't see is more important than what you can see. Only problem is… you can't see it.

MACDOUGALL

Makes sense to me.

SHAMUS

Did you know Dumpty?

MACDOUGALL

We had a few brushes. Dumpty was always a little hard boiled for my taste. Always playing the angles. Looking for the quick buck. Sometimes people got hurt. Sometimes they complained.

SHAMUS

Any of the good citizens of Peppermint Bay angry enough to to use the sidewalk for a frying pan?

MACDOUGALL

It'd be easier to make a list of everyone who didn't want to poach him.

SHAMUS

Any next of kin you know of?

MACDOUGALL

Last I heard he was hooked up with a singer over in Happy Valley.

SHAMUS

I might want to look her up.

MACDOUGALL

Hear she's a real looker.

SHAMUS

Then I'll definitely want to look her up. What's the canary's name?

72.

MACDOUGALL

Rapunzel.

SHAMUS

Did you say Rapunzel?

(DRAMATIC MUSIC STING)

MACDOUGALL

Yeah, that's what I said. Rapunzel.

(DRAMATIC MUSIC STING)

SHAMUS

That's what I thought you said.

MACDOUGALL

Then why did you make me repeat it.

SHAMUS

Dramatic emphasis.

(DRAMATIC MUSIC STING)

SHAMUS

Where can I find this Rapunzel?

MACDOUGALL

Works at a dive called Jack Sprat's out on Happy Valley Road. You can't miss it. It's on...

SHAMUS

I know. The edge of town.

(OMINOUS MUSIC STING)

SHAMUS

I decided to start with the thrush. In my experience, nine times outta ten, a guy gets scrambled, it's usually a dame handlin' the whisk.

(LOW CROWD NOISE)

RAPUNZEL
(sings in a low,
breathy voice like
Julie London)

Little Miss Muffet... She sat on her... tuffet, eating her curds and whey. When along came that big, bad spider, and sat down beside her. And frightened poor, little Miss Muffet away.

(APPLAUSE)

RAPUNZEL
Thank you, thank you. Stick around. I'll be back in five.

SHAMUS
Hello, Rapunzel.

RAPUNZEL
Well, well, well. If isn't Dick Shamus, the famous fictional flatfoot.

SHAMUS
Nice alliteration.

RAPUNZEL
I try.

SHAMUS
Rapunzel was one of those dames who always had lousy luck with men. When I first knew her she was hooked up with an ugly little half-pint named Rupelstilskin. Nobody could ever figure what she saw in the creep. But, then again, trying to figure out a dame was like trying to unravel quantum physics while banging your head on a wall. Either way, all you end up with is bunch of formulas and a headache.

RAPUNZEL
You done with the metaphors?

SHAMUS
For now.

RAPUNZEL
What brings you all the way out here, Shamus?

SHAMUS
I don't know how to tell you this.

RAPUNZEL
Why don't you try stringing a few verbs and nouns together until they form a complete sentence.

SHAMUS
Sensitive human being that I am, I broke the news as gently as I could. Dumpty's dead.

RAPUNZEL
Too bad. How'd the little ovum buy it?

SHAMUS
Fell off a wall. Had a great fall.

RAPUNZEL
Doesn't make sense.

74.

                         SHAMUS
Why's that.

                         RAPUNZEL
He was an egg. You do the math.

                         SHAMUS
You don't seem too broken up about it.

                         RAPUNZEL
Dumpty and me weren't exactly sunny side up.

                         SHAMUS
Another dame?

                         RAPUNZEL
Doctor's orders. My cholesterol as outta sight.

                         SHAMUS
Did he seem different lately?

                         RAPUNZEL
How different could he be. He was an egg. They're two ninety eight a dozen.

                         SHAMUS
Where were you around one o'clock?

                         RAPUNZEL
Yeah. Sure. Hang it on ole Rapunzel. Just like the old days.

                         SHAMUS
Rapunzel and me had what you might call a love-hate relationship. She loved hating me and I hated... But that's another story for another time in another place during another episode about another case where...

                         (SOUND OF RAPUNZEL SLAPPING SHAMUS)

                         SHAMUS
Still pack a stiff left hook, I see. What was that for?

                         RAPUNZEL
You were running on.

                         SHAMUS
You like doing that, didn't ya?

                         RAPUNZEL
As much as you liked me doing it.

                    SHAMUS
She was right. I did like it. There was something about
getting socked in the jaw by a gorgeous dame that made you
feel alive. Rapunzel, I didn't come out here to reminisce
about the good old days.

                    RAPUNZEL
Then why did you come out here?

                    SHAMUS
Dumpty called my office. Said he needed my help. You
wouldn't know about what, would ya?

                    RAPUNZEL
Beats me.

                    SHAMUS
If you think of anything let me know.

                    RAPUNZEL
I'll do that. If I think of anything.

                    SHAMUS
It was good seeing Rapunzel again. She was looking good.
Very good. Maybe after I'd wrapped things up here in
Peppermint Bay I'd drop in, buy her drink, catch up on old
times, rekindle the spark, light a fire. That is if she
wasn't the one who pushed Dumpty off the wall. If that was
the case, then I might have to rethink my priorities. And I
hate redoing my priorities. I decided to head back to
Peppermint Bay.

                    (A VOICE "PSSSSTING" SHAMUS)

                    SHAMUS
You pssssssting me?

                    ELF
There's only the two of us. Who else would I be pssssting?
Judy Garland?

                    SHAMUS
He stood about three feet high, wearing a red tunic, blue
tights and a yellow cloth cap that came to a point and then
tilted over to one side. What can I do for you?

                    ELF
You Shamus? The fictional copper?

                    SHAMUS
I'm Shamus.

ELF
Dumpty talked about you. He talked about you a lot.

SHAMUS
You a friend of Dumpty?

ELF
Yeah. You could say that.

SHAMUS
I just did.

ELF
Dumpty was a good egg. Poor guy. Got a rough deal. Didn't deserve to get shoved off that wall.

SHAMUS
You think he was pushed?

ELF
Bound to happen if you knew Dumpty.

SHAMUS
Think he stuck his nose in where it's didn't belong?

ELF
Except for one thing.

SHAMUS
What's that?

ELF
He didn't have a nose.

SHAMUS
What makes you think Dumpty's swan dive wasn't an accident.

ELF
All I know is that Dumpty and Wolfe got into it big time.

SHAMUS
Wolfe?

ELF
Yeah... B.B. Wolfe.

SHAMUS
The blues singer.

ELF
No... That's B.B. King.

SHAMUS
Who's this Wolfe guy?

ELF
Runs everything worth running in Paradise Bay. Not a good idea to get on his bad side and he doesn't have a good side.

SHAMUS
Sounds like a rough character, alright. So, when did this Wolfe and Dumpty have their set to?

ELF
A couple of days before Dumpty cracked his shell.

SHAMUS
When I knew Dumpty he was always playing some angle. Any idea what he was workin' on?

ELF
He did say something about a big score. Said he was about to hit the jackpot with some rich guy.

SHAMUS
This rich guy have a name?

ELF
I'm sure he does. He's rich.

SHAMUS
By the way. Know what Dumpty and this Wolfe guy were arguing about?

ELF
No. Couldn't hear it over all the whistling.

SHAMUS
Whistling?

ELF
Yeah. We whistle while we work. Company regulations. We took it to the union, but so far nothing.

(MUSICAL TRANSITION. PHONE RINGING

EFFIE
Fictional Bureau Of Investigation. Effie, the incredibly adorable secretary speaking.

SHAMUS
Effie, it's me.

                    EFFIE
Oh, hi boss.

                    SHAMUS
I need you to check something for me.

                    EFFIE
Sure. What is it?

                    SHAMUS
I need a list of all the rich guys who live in Peppermint
Bay.

                    EFFIE
Rich guys, huh? Want me to bring it over personally?

                    SHAMUS
Not necessary.

                    EFFIE
It wouldn't be any bother.

                    SHAMUS
Just get me the info.

                    EFFIE
Killjoy.

                              (FILM NOIR SAXOPHONE RIFF)

                    PEEP
              (breathy voice)
Well, hello there tall, dark and three dimensional

                    SHAMUS
She was the kind of girl that made a man glad she was that
kind of girl. And just who might you be?

                    PEEP
The name's Peep. Bo Peep.

                    SHAMUS
And what's a girl like you doing out here all by your
lonesome?

                    PEEP
I've lost my sheep.

                    SHAMUS
Your sheep?

                    PEEP
My sheep. And I don't know where to find them.

                    SHAMUS
Maybe I can help. I'm good at finding things.

                    PEEP
I'm all ears.

                    SHAMUS
If I were you, I'd leave them alone.

                    PEEP
Leave them alone?

                    SHAMUS
And they'll come home.

                    PEEP
Come home?

                    SHAMUS
And, not only that, they'll be wagging their tails behind them.

                    PEEP
And when you come home...

                    SHAMUS
Yeah?

                    PEEP
Will you be wagging your tail?

                    PEEP
You can count on it.

                    (MUSIC PLAYS HER OFF)

                    SHAMUS
Now, you may be asking, what's a drop dead beautiful dame in a tiny, little shepherdess outfit have to do with my case? The quick answer would be "Who cares?" But stick around. She'll be back. And, trust me, she'll play a very important part in the story.

                    MACDOUGALL
You wanted to see me laddie?

                    SHAMUS
You ever hear of a mug call himself B.B. Wolfe?

80.

MACDOUGALL
Who hasn't? Runs a mining operation not far from here. It's an unusual combination of exotic cuisine and open hole quarrying. You can enjoy a fine escargot while watching little men with lights on their head haul heavy rocks out of the ground.

SHAMUS
Where I can find this operation?

MACDOUGALL
It's just off Happy Valley Highway. You can't miss it. It's on... ..

SHAMUS
I know... The edge of town.

(OMINOUS MUSICAL STING)

WOLFE
(Gruff, tough voice)
The other way. It goes the other way. And you wonder why everyone calls you Dopey.

SHAMUS
Excuse me. I'm looking a B.B. Wolfe.

WOLFE
Who's askin'?

SHAMUS
I flashed my badge. I found it saved a lot of time and needless conversation.

WOLFE
What's that?

SHAMUS
My badge.

WOLFE
Badge? For what?

SHAMUS
For who I am and what I do.

WOLFE
Who are you and what do you do?

SHAMUS
The name's Shamus. Dick Shamus. F.B.I.

                              WOLFE

F.B.I?

                              SHAMUS
The Fictional Bureau of Investigation. I handle the
toughest, dirtiest crimes in English literature.

                              WOLFE
That means...

                              SHAMUS
That's right. I'm a fictional detective.

                              WOLFE
Why didn't you say so in the first place? We coulda saved a
lot of time and needless conversation.

                              SHAMUS
You Wolfe?

                              WOLFE
I'm Wolfe.

                              SHAMUS
You familiar with the name Dumpty?

                              WOLFE
Should I be?

                              SHAMUS
Let me tell you how this works, pal. I ask the questions.
You give the answers.

                              WOLFE
What was the question?

                              SHAMUS
See you did it again. You asked a question. Let's try it one
more time. You ever hear of a guy named Dumpty?

                              WOLFE
First name or last name?

                              SHAMUS
See, that's not an answer. That's another question. An
answer's got a period at the end. A question is followed by
a rising inflection and a squiggly thing. So I'll ask you
one more time. What were you and Dumpty arguing about?

                              WOLFE
What else do guys argue about?

                        SHAMUS
You mean a skirt? A Betty? A frail?

                        WOLFE
By that do you mean a girl?

                        SHAMUS
You could put it that way. It just wouldn't be as colorful.
What was the beef?

                        WOLFE
Dumpty didn't like the way I was lookin' at his old lady and
he didn't like the way she was lookin' at me.

                        SHAMUS
And how was she looking at you?

                        WOLFE
Sorta like this.

                        SHAMUS
Wolfe demonstrated by putting one hand behind his head and
the other hand on his hip in a pose that was supposed to
evoke the image of a flirtatious female, but instead looked
like a guy having back spasms. And how were you looking at
her?

                    (SOUNDS OF HEAVY PANTING)

                        WOLFE
Are we done here?

                        SHAMUS
We're done.

                        WOLFE
Good, cause I gotta go evict some old broad from a hush
puppy.

                        SHAMUS
If anyone could push Dumpty off a wall without a second
thought it was Wolfe. But then again, he was too obvious. A
guy like Wolfe would never do the deed himself. Unless he
didn't want anybody to have something to hang over his head.
Then he'd do it himself. Unless he didn't have a reason to
dump Dumpty. Although they did have a dust up over Rapunzel.
That'd be a reason. A good reason. Right now I was puttin'
Wolfe at the top of my list. Of course, if he didn't do it,
then I'd have to redo my list. And I hate redoing my list.

                      (PHONE RINGING)

EFFIE
EFFIE: Fictional Bureau Of Investigation, Effie, the incredibly available secretary speaking.

SHAMUS
Effie, it's me.

EFFIE
Oh, hi boss.

SHAMUS
Did you find anything on rich guys in Peppermint Bay?

EFFIE
There's only one who qualifies as rich.

SHAMUS
Just one?

EFFIE
Apparently there's not a lot of money in being a story book character. It seems everyone in Peppermint Bay is as poor as church mice. Especially the church mice.

SHAMUS
What's the name of Mister Moneybags?

EFFIE
Midas. Mitchell Midas. Everyone in Peppermint Bay calls him King.

SHAMUS
How'd make his bundle.

EFFIE
Mufflers.

SHAMUS
Car parts?

EFFIE
No. The kind you wrap around your neck.

SHAMUS
Thanks, doll

EFFIE
What are you going to now?

SHAMUS
I think it's time I paid Mister Moneybags a visit.

(MUSICAL TRANSITION)

SHAMUS
Officer MacDougall.

MACDOUGALL
Mister Shamus.

SHAMUS
Know anything about a Mitchell Midas?

MACDOUGALL
King Midas. Married. One daughter. Ran off about a year ago.

SHAMUS
Midas or the daughter?

MACDOUGALL
The daughter. Midas spent a fortune trying to find her.

SHAMUS
Any luck?

MACDOUGALL
Everyone figured she didn't want to be found.

SHAMUS
Where can I find this Midas?

MACDOUGALL
Lives on top of Midas Mountain. You can't miss it. It's on...

SHAMUS
I know... The edge of town.

(OMINOUS MUSIC STING)

SHAMUS
It turned out Midas lived in a cozy little bungalow. If your idea of cozy is the Taj Mahal. I rang the doorbell.

(CASH REGISTER SOUND. DOOR OPENING)

VERONICA
Well, well, well. Dick Shamus. I heard you were in town.

SHAMUS
Veronica. Veronice Virago. What are you doing here?

VERONICA
For one thing I live here. And for another thing the name isn't Veronica Virago. It's Midas.

SHAMUS
Midas Virago?

VERONICA
No. Veronica Midas. Mrs. Veronica Midas.

SHAMUS
In that case, I'm here to see your husband.

VERONICA
I'm afraid he's not seeing visitors.

SHAMUS
He'll want to see me.

VERONICA
My husband won't be seeing you or anyone else for that matter.

SHAMUS
You mean he's...

VERONICA
That's exactly what I mean.

SHAMUS
He's tied up on the phone.

VERONICA
No, that's not what I mean.

SHAMUS
He's away on business.

VERONICA
No, not that either.

SHAMUS
Then you mean he's...

VERONICA
Dead.

SHAMUS
My next guess would've been in the shower.

VERONICA
Then you would have been wrong.

SHAMUS
How'd he go?

                    VERONICA
Quietly.

                    SHAMUS
Was his death expected?

                    VERONICA
Not by him.

                    SHAMUS
Old age? Heart condition?

                    VERONICA
Suicide.

                    SHAMUS
Sleeping pills? Drowning.

                    VERONICA
Three bullets in the back.

                    SHAMUS
He must have been a helluva shot. Funny how all your husbands turn up face down.

                    VERONICA
What can I tell ya? I just can't catch a break.

                    SHAMUS
How many does that make? Five? Six?

                    VERONICA
Seven, but who's counting?

                    SHAMUS
When did he check out?

                    VERONICA
Last week.

                    SHAMUS
About the time Dumpty called. I wondered if it was a coincidence or just a situation in which events happen at the same time in a way that is not planned or expected?

                    VERONICA
Done wondering?

                    SHAMUS
Yeah.

                    VERONICA
Who's Dumpty?

SHAMUS
An old acquaintance. I'm looking into his death. Maybe you know him. William Jefferson Dumpty. But everyone called him Humpty.

VERONICA
Never heard of him.

SHAMUS
Funny, I think he might have been working for your late husband.

VERONICA
A lot of people worked for my late husband. And none of them were funny.

SHAMUS
I think Dumpty had some info on your missing daughter

VERONICA
Daughter??? Daughter??? Do I look like a person who would actually give birth?

SHAMUS
Okay, stepdaughter.

VERONICA
You're barking up the wrong tree. The kid hated her old men. She was always taking off and he was always bringing her back. Frankly, I never knew why.

SHAMUS
Maybe he loved her. Maybe he cared about. Something you'd no nothing about.

VERONICA
Listen to you. Always the do gooder. Protecting the weak. Defending the innocent. Looking out for the downtrodden.

SHAMUS
What would you know about the weak and innocent? You always were self centered, greedy, grasping, rapacious, avaricious and ravenous. In short she was everything I found irresistible in a woman.

VERONICA
You disgust me.

SHAMUS
You revolt me.

VERONICA
Oh yeah?

SHAMUS
Yeah.

VERONICA
Then why don't you do something about it.

SHAMUS
What do you suggest?

VERONICA
(passionately)
Kiss me.

(MUSIC TRANSITION)

SHAMUS
You had to hand it to Veronica. Sure she was evil, corrupt, and unprincipled but she was still a great kisser. Maybe when I'd wrapped things up here in Peppermint Bay I'd drop in, buy her drink, catch up on old times, rekindle the spark, light a fire. That is if she wasn't the one who pushed Dumpty off the wall. In that case I might have to rethink my priorities. And like I said, I hate rethinking my priorities.

(PHONE RINGING)

EFFIE
Fictional Bureau of Investigation. Effie, the incredibly delightful secretary speaking.

SHAMUS
It's me.

EFFIE
Oh, hi boss.

SHAMUS
I need you to track down Midas's will. I want to know what's in it. Who gets his geetus?

EFFIE
You mean when he dies?

SHAMUS
He's already done that.

EFFIE
I'm sorry to hear that.

SHAMUS
Not as sorry as he is.

89.

                    EFFIE
Oh, boss. Before you hang up. There's one more thing. It
seemed Midas owned a bunch of shell companies.

                    SHAMUS
He was in the sea shell business?

                    EFFIE
No shell companies. A company that has no or nominal
operations and no or normal assets consisting solely of cash
and cash equivalents or assets consisting of any amount of
cash and cash equivalents and other nominal assets.

                    SHAMUS
Okay, I get it. What I don't get is why I should care?

                    EFFIE
One of those shell companies owns a castle.

                    SHAMUS
What do you mean "a castle?"

                    EFFIE
You know. One of those places with a drawbridge, a moat and
a dragon.

                    SHAMUS
Lots of rich guys own castles.

                    EFFIE
But this castle is located just outside Peppermint Bay.
According to the records, no one's lived in it for years.

                    SHAMUS
That is interesting. Very interesting.

                    (TRANSITIONAL MUSIC)

                    MACDOUGALL
You wanted to see me, Mister Shamus?

                    SHAMUS
Is there a castle around here?

                    MACDOUGALL
Are you kidding? This place is lousy with castles. You can't
swing a dead cat in the hat without hitting one.

                    SHAMUS
How about one that hasn't been occupied for years? One that
people might have forgotten about.

MACDOUGALL
Yeah... Yeah. A forgotten castle. I do remember something about a forgotten castle.

SHAMUS
Know where it is?

MACDOUGALL
I forget.

SHAMUS
That's good enough for me. Meet me back here in three hours. And bring a large bag of bread crumbs.

MACDOUGALL
Why? You planning on cooking a cutlet?

SHAMUS
And one more thing. Deliver these three envelopes for me.

(TRANSITIONAL MUSIC)

SHAMUS
We've been walking for hours MacDougall. And no castle in sight.

MACDOUGALL
Feels like we're going around in circles, laddie. I hate to say this, but I think we're lost.

SHAMUS
Don't worry Mack. When you've been in the fictional detective business as long as I have you realize that this is what they call a "tension builder."

MACDOUGALL
If you don't mind asking, what's a tension builder?

SHAMUS
Simple. It's usually comes around this point in the story. It's when the detective in question, right now me, has a revelation that only he knows but he's not telling anyone about. Unfortunately, I'm not havin' one of those revelations.

MACDOUGALL
What do we do now?

SHAMUS
It's time for plan B.

MACDOUGALL
Not plan B. I hate plan B.

                              SHAMUS
Don't worry. Plan B in this case is a clue showin' up out of
nowhere, that'll get us back on track. It isn't the most
satisfying literary device and usually demonstrates a
complete lack of imagination.

                    (SOUNDS OF THUNDER AND RAIN)

                              SHAMUS
But any plot twist in a storm.

                              MACDOUGALL
Shamus.

                              SHAMUS
What?

                              MACDOUGALL
Look. That sign.

                              SHAMUS
What sign?

                              MACDOUGALL
The one that reads "Abandoned Castle This Way."

                              SHAMUS
Mac, you're a genius. Let's go. There's no time to waste.

                    *(UPBEAT MUSIC. SOUND OF
                    CREAKING DOOR)*

                              SHAMUS
                         (his voice echoing)
Man, this place is big.

                              ECHO
Big... Big... Big.

                              SHAMUS
I'm sure, she's got be here.

                              ECHO
Here... Here... Here.

                              MACDOUGALL
Who?

                              ECHO
Who? Who? Who?

                              SHAMUS
The missing frail.

ECHO
Frail... Frail... Frial.

MACDOUGALL
Let's try these stairs. They lead to the keep?

ECHO
Keep... Keep... Keep.

(FOOTSTEPS)

MACDOUGALL
Be careful laddie. These steps are steep.

ECHO
Steep... Steep... Steep.

(CREAKING DOOR. SOUND OF GENTLE SNORING)

SHAMUS
It's her. She's asleep.

ECHO
Asleep... Asleep... Asleep.

MACDOUGALL
Looks kinda sweet.

ECHO
Sweet... Sweet... Sweet.

SHAMUS
Like a young Meryl Streep.

ECHO
(annoyed)
Meryl Streep??? Meryl Streep??? That's the best you can do? Meryl Streep? You guys are pathetic. I'm outta here.

SHAMUS
Put that blanket over her for now.

MACDOUGALL
Okay. Now what?

SHAMUS
We wait.

MACDOUGALL
For what?

                    SHAMUS
Our prime suspects.

                    RAPUNZEL
Shamus.

                    SHAMUS
Rapunzel. Glad you could make it.

                    RAPUNZEL
So you're the one who sent the note.

                    SHAMUS
That's right.

                    RAPUNZEL
And laid down that trail of bread crumbs.

                    SHAMUS
Right again.

                    RAPUNZEL
What was the whole idea of having them go round in circles?

                    SHAMUS
                 (annoyed)
Never mind the bread crumbs.

                    RAPUNZEL
What am I doing here?

                    SHAMUS
You'll find out in a minute.

                    WOLFE
Rapunzel?

                    RAPUNZEL
Wolfie?

                    WOLFE
What are you doing here?

                    RAPUNZEL
What are you doing here?

                    WOLFE
I gotta note. Said to follow the bread crumbs.

                    SHAMUS
I sent that note.

WOLFE
I'd've got here sooner but the trail kept going around in circles. What was that all about?

SHAMUS
(more annoyed)
Forget the bread crumbs.

WOLFE
What are we doing here?

SHAMUS
We're waiting for one more... Veronica. Right on cue.

WOLFE
What's she doing here?

VERONICA
I gotta note.

RAPUNZEL
You too?

VERONICA
I'm guessing it was you Shamus.

SHAMUS
That was me alright.

VERONICA
So why the bread crumbs going round in circles?

SHAMUS
(really annoyed)
Forget the bread crumbs.

WOLFE
What are we all doing here Shamus?

SHAMUS
One of you pushed Dumpty off that wall. And we're here to reveal which one it is.

RAPUNZEL
Well, I didn't do it.

WOLFE
And I didn't do it.

VERONICA
I didn't even know the guy.

                        SHAMUS
Before we get around to Dumpty's killer, there's one other
piece of business to clear up first. Mack, pull back the
blanket.
                    (gentle snoring)
The sweet, lovely, young woman, snoring her brains out is
the key to the mystery of who killed Humpty Dumpty.

                        WOLFE
What can she tell us?

                        SHAMUS
Who drugged her and why.

                        RAPUNZEL
She looks like she's in some kind of coma.

                        SHAMUS
Now, Mac, what was it about you told me about the legend
when we found the girl?

                        MACDOUGALL
That the only way to wake her was with a kiss.

                        SHAMUS
And what did I tell you?

                        MACDOUGALL
That wakin' gorgeous dames with a kiss wasn't exactly your
style. That you preferred to slip out quietly while they
were still in dreamland.

                        SHAMUS
And what did you tell me would happen after the girl was
kissed?

                        MACDOUGALL
That she'd wake up, fall in love with the man who kissed
her, marry him and live happily ever after?

                        SHAMUS
And what did I ask you?

                        MACDOUGALL
Which is it? Marry or live happily ever after?

                        SHAMUS
And what did you say?

                        MACDOUGALL
Both.

                              SHAMUS
And what did I say?

                            MACDOUGALL
That's no legend. That's a fairy tale.

                              SHAMUS
The girl is the key to this case. And to unlock that key, I
am going to make the ultimate sacrifice and wake her up with
a kiss. If she falls madly in love with me, so be it. She
won't be the first.

                      RAPUNZEL/WOLFE/VERONICA
Stop!!!

                              SHAMUS
That was a close call. So all of you have a reason for this
young girl to remain comatose. You wanna go first Rapunzel?
I'm guessing Dumpty had something on you. Something about
the girl you didn't want anyone to know.

                             RAPUNZEL
Okay. It's true. He found out my secret. Bambi is my
daughter.

                              SHAMUS
Who the hell is Bambi?

                             RAPUNZEL
That's her name. Dumpty told me he knew where she was, but
he was going to sell the information to Midas for big bucks.

                              SHAMUS
So the girl was really Midas's daughter.

                              WOLFE
No. She's my daughter.

                              SHAMUS
Wait a minute. Rapunzel says the girl is her daughter. You
say she's your daughter. Which is it?

                              WOLFE
Both.

                              SHAMUS
How is that possible?

                              WOLFE
Well, you see Shamus, when a man loves a woman...

                              SHAMUS
You and Rapunzel?

WOLFE
I know. Hard to believe. Bambi doesn't look a thing like me.

SHAMUS
Thank heavens for that. So how did she end up with Midas?

RAPUNZEL
When me and Wolfie first got together we were kids ourselves. Poorer than church mice.

WOLFE
I'd just started the loan sharking business.

RAPUNZEL
And don't forget the protection racket.

WOLFE
I almost forgot about that. So Midas agreed to look after Bambi until we could get on our feet.

SHAMUS
What happened?

WOLFE
Once I started bribing politicians and the money began rolling in...

RAPUNZEL
Bambi was growing up. And she looked so happy...

WOLFE
We didn't have the heart to take her away from the life she had known.

SHAMUS
Why Mitchell Midas?

WOLFE
He was my brother.

VERONICA
That's a lie. He never talked about a brother.

WOLFE
He was my brother from a another mother.

SHAMUS
So that's what you and Dumpty were arguing about that day. So, all of you had a motive.

VERONICA
We know about these two. What about me?

SHAMUS
We're gonna get to that.

MACDOUGALL
Please laddie. Not a long, boring speech summing up who did what and when that is so convoluted nobody can follow it.

SHAMUS
Try and stop me. It all goes back to Midas's will. It leaves everything to sleeping beauty here. Unless, for some reason, the girl is still alive but out of commission. Then Veronica gets to run the show and spend the dough. Am I going to fast for ya?

VERONICA
Sorry, I was checking my email.

SHAMUS
But if the girl turns up dead, then the geetus goes to charity. And Veronica ends up with the clothes on her back. If she can keep them on her back. So just to be safe, Veronica, you drugged the girl and stashed her here where no one could find her. When Dumpty contacted Midas to set up a meet to sell him info on the girl's whereabouts, you found out about it. You lured Dumpty to the top of the wall and pushed him off. You thought you were in the clear until I showed up. You'd knew I'd figure out what happened because I always do. And you knew I'd tell Midas cause that's the kind of guy I am. So before I could figure out what happened, tell Midas and watch him toss you out in the cold, you put three bullets in his back and called it suicide.

VERONICA
Shamus, you're just whistling Dixie.

SHAMUS
That's where you're wrong, Veronica. I never learned to whistle.

VERONICA
You can't prove any of this.

SHAMUS
I don't have to. All I have to do is wake up the girl with a kiss. And she'll tell us who drugged her.

VERONICA
Stop.

WOLFE
Be careful, Shamus. She has a magic wand.

VERONICA
All I have to do is say the magic words...

SHAMUS
Just put down the magic wand Veronica and no one gets hurt.

VERONICA
We're done talking. Goodbye Shamus. Salagadoola meshugina boola...

MACDOUGALL
Be careful, laddie.

VERONICA
Salagadoola mechicka boola...

SHAMUS
You were saying Veronica.

VERONICA
Stay back. Salagadoola ...Boppity hoppity... Bibbidi... Yibbidi... Damn.

(SOUND OF VERONICA RUNNING)

WOLFE
She's on the run.

SHAMUS
We can't let her get away.

WOLFE
Rapunzel, stay here with Bambi.

RAPUNZEL
Be careful, Wolfie. Remember what the vet said about your heart.

VERONICA
Salagadoola chicka chicka boom boom.

(SOUNDS OF RUNNING)

MACDOUGALL
Over here, Shamus.

VERONICA
Boola boola. Boola boola.

SHAMUS
Mack. Raise the drawbridge.

MACDOUGALL
Wolfe. Lower the portocullis.

WOLFE
Sure. No problem. The portocullis. What's a portocullus?

VERONICA
Salagadoola something something.

SHAMUS
She's upstairs.

WOLFE
She's downstairs.

MACDOUGALL
She's in my lady's chamber.

SHAMUS
You might as well give up, Veronica. We've got you surrounded. Throw out the magic wand and come out with your hands up.

MACDOUGALL
Good work, laddie.

VERONICA
That's the last time I buy a magic wand off Ebay.

PRINCE CHARMING
Excuse me.

SHAMUS
Who the heck are you?

PRINCE CHARMING
(all arrogance)
Who am I? Who am I?

SHAMUS
Yeah, that was the question. Who are you?

PRINCE CHARMING
Why, my good man, I am every girl's dream come true.

SHAMUS
Ain't we all.

PRINCE CHARMING
I am... Prince Charming.

SHAMUS
Mind telling us how you got here, Prince?.

PRINCE CHARMING
I followed this trail of bread crumbs. I would have gotten here sooner but it kept going around in these circles.

SHAMUS
(really, really annoyed)
Forge the bread crumbs. What are you doing here?

PRINCE CHARMING
I have come to wake the sleeping beauty with a kiss.

SHAMUS
Fine with me. But before you lay one on her, you better check with mom and dad.

RAPUNZEL
Are you a real prince?

PRINCE CHARMING
Of course, I am.

WOLFE
You got some I.D?

PRINCE CHARMING
Will this crown do?

RAPUNZEL
Knock yourself out.

PRINCE CHARMING
With this kiss I will awaken the sleeping beauty from her slumber.

(LONG, LOUD SMOOCH)

RAPUNZEL
With that kiss, he could wake the dead.

SLEEPING BEAUTY
(waking up)
Oh... Oh... Where am I? And who are you?

SHAMUS
The name's Shamus.

SLEEPING BEAUTY
Are you my Prince Charming?

SHAMUS
No. He is.

SLEEPING BEAUTY
(disappointed)

Oh...

PRINCE CHARMING
Will you marry me and be my princess?

SLEEPING BEAUTY
I don't know. This is all so sudden. If I marry you will we live happily ever after?

PRINCE CHARMING
Yes. Yes. We will

SLEEPING BEAUTY
In a big castle?

PRINCE CHARMING
In a very big castle.

SLEEPING BEAUTY
With beautiful gowns to wear.

PRINCE CHARMING
With the most beautiful gowns you've ever seen.

SLEEPING BEAUTY
And no pre-nup?

PRINCE CHARMING
And no pre-nup.

SLEEPING BEAUTY
And...?

RAPUNZEL
I wouldn't push your luck, sweetie.

SLEEPING BEAUTY
In that case, it works for me.

PRINCE CHARMING
You have made me the happiest man in the world.

SHAMUS
Has he got a lot to learn. It all worked out in the end. Rapunzel and Wolfe were back together. Bambi married her prince. And as for Veronica... Mack, you can take her away.

MACDOUGALL
With pleasure, laddie. With pleasure

                    VERONICA
You haven't heard the last of me Shamus.

                    SHAMUS
Hate to bust your bubble, Veronica. But there ain't gonna be
a sequel.

                    VERONICA
Damn.

                    (SEXY SAXOPHONE MUSIC)

                    PEEP
Oh, Shamus...

                    SHAMUS
Peep.

                    PEEP
My sheep came home just like you said. Now it's your turn.

                    SHAMUS
Well, as for me... I lived happily ever after. I told you
the girl would play an important part in the story.

                    (HAPPY ENDING MUSIC)

                    ANNOUNCER
You've been listening to "The Adventures of Dick Shamus,
Fictional Detective." Tune in next week for another episode
from the files of "Dick Shamus, Fictional Detective

                    (MUSIC UP AND OUT

                    THE END

"ALIAS CINDERELLA"

A DICK SHAMUS MYSTERY

by Bruce Kane

("Alias Cinderella" is copyrighted material and may not be presented or produced without written permission of Bruce Kane Productions. You may request a royalty free license at kaneprod.com/contact.htm.)

> *(CAST ENTERS, SCRIPTS IN HAND ACTORS WILL APPROACH THE MICROPHONES AT THE APPROPRIATE MOMENTS)*

STAGE MANAGER
We go in five... four... three... two...

> *(The Stage Manager points. Bluesy film noir saxophone is heard.)*

SHAMUS
The name's Shamus. Dick Shamus. I work for the F.B.I. The Fictional Bureau of Investigation. I handle the toughest, dirtiest cases in English literature. That's right, I'm a fictional detective.

> *(Saxophone out. After a beat, stirring music up and under)*

ANNOUNCER
It's the Adventures of Dick Shamus, Fictional Detective starring Jason Tindal as Dick Shamus, Fictional Detective. Tonight's episode "Alias Cinderella."

SHAMUS
After two weeks on stakeout, I was looking forward to a little R and R. That would be Rhonda and Rosalie. But that dream was soon ended when Effie, my long suffering secretary, told me there was someone waiting to see me.

EFFIE
There's some guy waitin' to see you. I think he's a prince or a king or somethin'.

SHAMUS
What makes you think he's a prince or a king or somethin'?

EFFIE
How many guys you know go around wearing a crown?

SHAMUS

That would be a dead giveway, alright. Let's not keep his majesty waiting. Send him him.

EFFIE

The boss'll see you now.

(SFX: FOOTSTEPS)

LACKEY

Presenting his royal highness, Prince Alfonse William Robert Hastings Oxford Jonathan Milford Anthony Phillip William... again...

SHAMUS

Was there a name this guy didn't have?

LACKEY

Albert Constantine Charming. Prince of Lyman on Twill, Hutchings on Vetch, Twicky on Guss and Ham on Rye.

PRINCE

Thank you, Lumpy.

LACKEY

Lackey, sir. It's Lackey.

PRINCE

I gather by the lettering on that shabby door in that shabby hall outside this shabby office, that you are Shamus.

SHAMUS

At least, the guy could read. More than you can say for most of these inbreds.

PRINCE

I am told that you are very good at finding things.

SHAMUS

You were told right.

PRINCE

Good. I want you to find a girl.

SHAMUS

This ain't a dating service, Prince.

PRINCE

I want you to find a missing girl.

SHAMUS

In that case... does this missing girl have a name?

PRINCE
I'm sure she does.

SHAMUS
But you don't know what it is. Okay, then, know where she lives?

PRINCE
No idea.

SHAMUS
A real fountain of information, ain't ya?. Can you give me anything?

PRINCE
Lindy, the shoe.

LACKEY
Lackey, sir. It's Lackey.

PRINCE
Of course it is. The shoe.

SHAMUS
A shoe? That's all you got? A shoe?

PRINCE
Not just any shoe, Mr. Shamus.

SHAMUS
The prince was right about that. It wasn't just any shoe. It was...

PRINCE
(dramatically)
A glass slipper.

SHAMUS
Sounds uncomfortable. But when it came to a dame's shoes, I learned long ago...comfort was not the primary purpose. Tell you what prince, why don't you tell me the whole story. And don't leave out any details.

PRINCE
It happened the night before last. I'd thrown a big costume ball at the palace. Everyone who was anyone was there.

SHAMUS
I wasn't.

PRINCE
Yes. Like I said, everyone was anyone.

SHAMUS
Tell me more.

PRINCE
Across the room my eyes came to rest on this vision in white. She was sweet, lovely, innocent. So I did what any self respecting prince would do.

SHAMUS
I can't wait.

PRINCE
I sent Lumpy here...

LACKEY
That's Lackey, sir. Lackey.

PRINCE
I sent him over to make the introductions.

LACKEY
Presenting his royal highness Alfonse William Robert Hastings Oxford Jonathan..

SHAMUS
I get it. I get it.

PRINCE
I asked the young lady if she would like to dance. She agreed. We talked. We danced. We smiled. We danced... We laughed. We...

SHAMUS
Can we move this along before it turns into "Dancing With The Stars?"

PRINCE
The clock began to chime out the midnight hour.

LACKEY
Bong...bong...bong...

SHAMUS
You can lose the sound effects, Lumpy.

LACKEY
Lackey. That's Lackey.

PRINCE
And then, for no apparent reason I could discern she took off like a bat out of you know where.

SHAMUS
That's it?

PRINCE
That's it. When I raced after her, the only left behind was this glass slipper.

SHAMUS
That's one helluva shoe, Prince.

PRINCE
She was one helluva girl.

SHAMUS
Can you describe her? What did she look like?

PRINCE
Aside from possessing shoulders carved from the finest alabaster, a smile as fresh as a morning sunrise and a body like a brick pagoda, I couldn't say.

SHAMUS
What do you mean, you couldn't say?

PRINCE
I couldn't say. She was wearing a mask.

SHAMUS
A mask? Was she that ugly?

PRINCE
We were all wearing masks. It was a masked ball. You don't get out much, do you Mr. Shamus?

SHAMUS
You're not giving me much to go on Prince.

PRINCE
If I had anything to go on, I wouldn't need you, would I?

SHAMUS
Missing dames ain't usually my specialty.

PRINCE
I'll pay you handsomely. Lampley, the gold.

LACKEY
That's Lackey, sir. Lackey.

PRINCE
Just give him the gold. I believe this will more than make up for you reticence, sir.

110.

                        SHAMUS

That's a lotta lettuce.

                        PRINCE

She's a lotta girl. Can I count on you Mr. Shamus?

                        SHAMUS

I'll see what I can do.

                        PRINCE

And I trust I can count on your discretion? If word ever got out I was searching for a girl, every young woman in the kingdom with shoulders carved from the finest alabaster, a smile as fresh as a morning sunrise and a body like a brick pagoda, would be lining up outside the castle gate offering who knows what for a chance to fit into that shoe.

                        SHAMUS

And we wouldn't want that, would we Prince?

                        PRINCE

It's not easy being me, Mr. Shamus. Let me know the minute you find her. I'm counting on you, Mr. Shamus. I'm counting on you.

                        (Footsteps. Door opening, door closing. Musical transition)

                        SHAMUS

There was something about this case that didn't smell right. It happens that way with some cases. There are some things the client tells you and then there are things the client doesn't tell you. Usually the things they don't tell you are more important than the things they do tell you. The only problem is... they didn't tell you.
                        (calls out)

Effie.

                        PRINCE

Yeah, boss?

                        SHAMUS

You're a girl.

                        EFFIE

It's been a long time since I was a "girl."

                        SHAMUS

Be that as it may, what can you tell me about this shoe?

                        EFFIE

It's expensive. I can tell you that.

                    SHAMUS
How expensive is expensive?

                    EFFIE
With what you pay me, I could live for a year on what this
one shoe costs.

                    SHAMUS
How can you tell?

                    EFFIE
Like you said. I'm a "girl." Besides, this shoe was made by
Manolo Gepetto. Says so right here. See? They don't pop
these out like gum balls. Every one is custom made.

                    SHAMUS
Do me a favor, see what you can dig up on this Gepetto
character.

                    EFFIE
What are you gonna do?

                    SHAMUS
See if I can find the dame that fits this shoe.

                (Musical transition)

                    SHAMUS
The girl I was looking for had shoulders carved from the
finest alabaster, a smile like a morning sunrise and a body
like a brick pagoda. I decided to start with the brick
pagoda. Excuse me.

                    WOMAN
Yes?

                    SHAMUS
How would you like to be princess?

                    MAN
Take it from me, pal. She's already a princess. C'mon
Sheila.

                    SHAMUS
Excuse me, toots.

                    WOMAN #2
Yes, what is it?

                    SHAMUS
Would you mind trying on this shoe for me?

WOMAN #2
That's a Manolo Gepetto isn't it?

SHAMUS
Yes, it is.

WOMAN #2
I'd love to.

SHAMUS
Here let me help you slip it on.

WOMAN #2
Oh, thank you.

SHAMUS
Say, you ever dance at Big Eddie's over on the southside?

WOMAN #2
No.

SHAMUS
You sure? I never forget a great set of gams.

EFFIE
Boss. Oh, there you are. I've been lookin' all for you.

SHAMUS
Hold on a sec. I'm busy here.

EFFIE
Busy or just tryin' to get busy.

SHAMUS
Sorry the shoe didn't fit, toots.

WOMAN #2
Not as sorry as I am.

SHAMUS
So, what'd you find out?

EFFIE
Manolo Gepetto. Makes one of a kind women's shoes and handbags. Says here he makes women's fantasies come true.

SHAMUS
What kind of fantasies?

EFFIE
What else? One a kind shoes and handbags.

(Transitional Music)

SHAMUS
When I got to Gepetto's workshop it turned out he wasn't in. Instead, I ran into a kid who was long on attitude with a nose to match. Hey you. Cyrano.

PINNOCHIO
A wise guy. What do you want, wise guy?

SHAMUS
A little information.

PINNOCHIO
You come to the right place. I got as little as you need.

SHAMUS
I'm looking for Manolo Gepetto. Is he around?

PINNOCHIO
Who wants to know?

SHAMUS
The name's Shamus. Dick Shamus. Now that you know my moniker, what's yours?

PINNOCHIO
Pinnochio... If you must know.

SHAMUS
Gepetto around?

PINNOCHIO
Never heard of him.

SHAMUS
You're lying kid. I don't know why you're lying, but you're lying. It's as plain as the nose on your face.

PINNOCHIO
Sure, sure. Okay, so you figured it out. Pin a rose on you.

SHAMUS
I had no idea what the kid was talking about.

PINNOCHIO
You think it's easy walking around with a lie detector in the middle of your face? It's a curse, man. How'd you like it if every time you told a lie, your nose grew an inch? It sucks, man.

SHAMUS
I bet.

PINNOCHIO
Especially when it comes to women.

SHAMUS
Dames can be a little "selective" when it comes to a guy's mug.

PINNOCHIO
That's not it. It's later. At first, it's all "You're so honest. So different from all the others guys I've dated." But it's always out there.

SHAMUS
The question.

PINNOCHIO
You got it, my man. The question. It's like this giant boulder that starts rolling right at you as soon as things start to get serious. And it just keeps rolling and rolling and rolling.

SHAMUS
Getting bigger and bigger.

PINNOCHIO
Every other guy in the world can fake his way through it by lying through his teeth. But not me. Not when she finally asks...

SHAMUS
The unanswerable question.

PINNOCHIO
Does this dress make me look fat?

SHAMUS
It's gotta be rough. I feel for you my friend. Nothin'll kill a relationship faster than the truth.

PINNOCHIO
Thanks for understanding. You're alright. What do you need?

SHAMUS
Recognize this shoe?

PINNOCHIO
It's one of ours. I made it myself.

SHAMUS
Who'd you make it for?

PINNOCHIO
Some woman called herself Lisa Condo came in a coupla months ago with this very hot young chick.

SHAMUS
How would you describe her?

PINNOCHIO
Like I said. Very hot.

SHAMUS
I mean the woman.

PINNOCHIO
Imagine the Wicked Witch of the West, minus the charm.

(Transitional music. Door opening)

EFFIE
Oh, hi boss.

SHAMUS
Were you able to find anything on that Lisa Condo dame?

EFFIE
Sells real estate on the West Side. Got a rap sheet as long as your... well, let's just say your arm.

SHAMUS
What kind of rap sheet?

EFFIE
You name it. Mail fraud, wire fraud, securities fraud, insurance fraud, bond fraud, check fraud, credit card fraud, medical fraud, online fraud, off line fraud, defensive line fraud and just plain old fashioned fraud fraud.

SHAMUS
Busy girl.

EFFIE
She's also got a list of aliases as long as your... Well, let's just say your arm. Ginger Snap, Helen Troy, Barbara Seville, Carrie Baggs, Isabell Ringing, Marsha Mellow, Anne Teak, May Day, and Anna Reksic.

(Dramatic music sting)

SHAMUS
Did you say Anna Reksic?

(Dramatic music sting)

                              EFFIE
That's what I said. Anna Reksic.

                              SHAMUS
That's what I thought you said.

                              EFFIE
Then why did you make me repeat it?

                              SHAMUS
Dramatic effect.

                                        (Dramatic music sting)

                              EFFIE
She an old friend of yours?

                              SHAMUS
If you wanna call someone who once tried to put a shiv in
your back, an old friend.

                                        *(Musical transition. Doorbell.
                                        Door opening)*

                              LISA
Well, well, well. If it isn't Dick Shamus, fictional dick.
How's tricks, Shamus?

                              SHAMUS
Can't complain. How about you Anna? Or is it Lisa, now?

                              LISA
Take your pick.

                              SHAMUS
Miss me?

                              LISA
The only time I missed you was when my gun jammed. So, do
what do I owe this visit?

                              SHAMUS
Recognize this shoe?

                              LISA
Should I?

                              SHAMUS
You ordered it. Special.

                              LISA
I order a lot of things. You should see my Amazon bill.

                         SHAMUS
You had this one custom made and another one just like it.

                         LISA
I ordered two right shoes? I don't think so.

                         SHAMUS
Well, not just like it. For the other foot.

                         LISA
In that case, thanks for returning it.

                         SHAMUS
This wasn't made for you.

                         LISA
What makes you say that?

                         SHAMUS
It's a petite. That's French for you couldn't wedge this on your foot with a block and tackle. Where's the girl?

                         LISA
What girl?

                         SHAMUS
The girl who goes with this shoe.

                         LISA
If you insist.
                    (calls out)
Ursulala.

                        URSULALA
                    (man faking high
                    female voice)
You called, stepmommy?

                         LISA
This is my stepdaughter, Ursulala. She's my fourth husband's fifth daughter. Or is it my fifth husband's fourth daughter? It's so hard to keep track these days.

                         SHAMUS
Nice try Lisa. But the girl I'm looking for possesses shoulders carved from the finest alabaster, a smile as fresh as a morning sunrise and a body like a brick pagoda. From where I stand Ursulala, here, is batting oh for three.

                        URSULALA
Oh mommy. That man is so mean.

LISA
It's okay, honey You can go to your room now. Stepmommy and Mr. Shamus have some business to discuss.

URSULALA
Yes, stepmommy.

SHAMUS
Okay, Lisa, what's the scam?

LISA
I'm just a hard working single mom trying to sell a little real estate. Perhaps I could interest you in a two bedroom apartment, completely refurbished, granite counter tops, fresh paint, new appliances, four tennis courts, three pools, two parking spaces and…?

SHAMUS
The only thing you're selling sweetheart is smoke and mirrors.

LISA
Oh. Then you've seen the place.

SHAMUS
You got something up your sleeve Lisa and sooner or later I'm gonna find out what it is.

LISA
If you wanna look up my sleeve Shamus, it's gonna cost you, at the very least, dinner and a movie.

(Transitional music)

SHAMUS
There were definitely two sides to this case. One was down and one was up. The downside? I was getting nowhere. The upside? I was getting there fast. But, what I didn't expect was the unexpected turn the case was about to take. That's the trouble with unexpected turns. They come when you least expect them.

(Door opening)

EFFIE
Hi boss... There's someone waiting for you.

SHAMUS
Anybody I know?

EFFIE
More like somebody you're gonna wanna know.

(Door opening)

CINDERELLA
(sweet, syrupy
southern, girlish
accent)
Are you Mistah Shamus?

SHAMUS
I'm Shamus. And who might you be?

CINDERELLA
I'm the girl you've been looking for.

SHAMUS
All my life or just recently?

CINDERELLA
The one the prince wants you to find.

SHAMUS
I've had a lot of applicants lately who think they can fill the shoe.

CINDERELLA
Shall we try?

SHAMUS
She extended a leg that would have gone on forever if it didn't have a foot attached to it.

CINDERELLA
Well, what do you think, Mistah Shamus?

SHAMUS
You don't want to know what I think.

CINDERELLA
I meant the shoe.

SHAMUS
Perfect fit. The prince is gonna be happy to see you again.

CINDERELLA
Oh no, Mr. Shamus. You musn't tell him. No, no, no. That's what I came to tell you. You mustn't keep lookin' for me. And you mustn't tell my wicked, wicked stepmother either.

SHAMUS
Wicked stepmother.

CINDERELLA
Wicked, wicked stepmother.

SHAMUS
Wicked, wicked stepmother?

CINDERELLA
Lisa Condo.

SHAMUS
Lisa Condo is your stepmother?

CINDERELLA
I'm her eighth husband's seventh daughter. Or her seventh husband's eighth daughter. Oh, fiddly dee, it's also so confusing for a poor little girl like me. If she found out I was talking to you, I shudder to think what she might do.

SHAMUS
Tell me everything, sweet knees.

CINDERELLA
It was all her idea. She made me do it.

SHAMUS
Made you do what?

CINDERELLA
She made me wear that form fitting ball gown by Donatella Versace. And the twenty carat, one a kind, diamond necklace with matching ear rings from Bulgari as well as the custom made shoes by Manolo Gepetto. It was awful Mr. Thyme. Just awful.

SHAMUS
I can imagine. What dame wants to go a fancy dress ball at the royal palace looking like Margot Robbie? It must have been torture. But why go to all the trouble?

CINDERELLA
She called it "baiting the hook."

SHAMUS
I'm guessing Prince Charming was the big fish she was out to land.

CINDERELLA
She said you were the cleverest man she'd ever met.

SHAMUS
For once in her life she was straight. Why'd you run away when you had the fish on the line?

CINDERELLA
That was part of the plan. Just engaging the prince for a night wasn't enough. It's just so embarrassing to even think about it.

SHAMUS
Please, go on.

CINDERELLA
Lisa wanted to pull him in deeper. Reel him into the boat, I think is how she put it. That's why I ran, Mr.Shamus, so he'd follow me and rescue me and marry me and...

SHAMUS
You'd both live happily ever after.

CINDERELLA
Oh, no, Mr. Shamus. Marry me, yes. But just so my wicked, wicked stepmother could move into the palace and drain the treasury dry. She was the one who was going to live happily ever after. She's wicked my stepmother. Wicked. She treats me mean terrible, Mr. Shamus. You should definitely do something about her before she makes some other poor, innocent girl do terrible, terrible things.

SHAMUS
Count on it. What are you going to do?

CINDERELLA
I am leaving Mr. Shamus. Leavin' for good. Goin' far, far away where no one will ever see me again.

SHAMUS
I could talk to the Prince. He seemed mighty interested.

CINDERELLA
Oh, no, Mr. Shamus. That wouldn't be fair to the Prince. Me not bein' who he thinks I am.

SHAMUS
Take it from me. He wouldn't care if you told him you we're Tilly from Hoboken. And he's still a prince.

CINDERELLA
Rich or poor, it doesn't matter. I just want a man to love me for who I am. Just a sweet, innocent girl with shoulders carved from the finest alabaster, a smile like a morning sunrise and a body like a brick pagoda.

SHAMUS
Where will you go?

CINDERELLA
Where I can be free. Free from wearin' rags, and scrubbin' floors and goin' to bed without my supper. As God is my witness, Mr. Shamus, I will nevah be hungry again.

SHAMUS
At least tell me your name.

CINDERELLA
O'Hara... Katie Cinderella O'Hara.

(Door closing)

SHAMUS
And with that she was gone. Gone with the wind. It was time to break the news to the Prince. Or so I thought. But unexpected turns have ways of turning up unexpectedly and this turn was really unexpected which would explain why I didn't expect it.

MAN
(struggling to speak)
Sham... Shamus...

(Body falling with a thud)

EFFIE
Boss, are you alright? He just pushed his way past me. I couldn't stop him.

SHAMUS
It's okay.

EFFIE
He's dead, isn't he?

SHAMUS
Either that or he's really good at holding his breath.

EFFIE
Murdered.

SHAMUS
What makes you think that?

EFFIE
For one thing, the knife in his back. Who is he?

SHAMUS
Ursulala.

EFFIE
Who?

SHAMUS
Lisa Condo's ugly stepdaughter.

EFFIE
I'll give you ugly. But that's no stepdaughter.

SHAMUS
I know this guy. He's part time muscle, sometime enforcer and full time Arthur Murray dance instructor.

EFFIE
Sounds versatile.

SHAMUS
Goes by the name of Vinny "The Mug" Bingbang. Also known as Vinny "The Slug", Vinny "The Bug" and once in a while Hobart T. Percywhistle. You'd better call the coroner. Tell 'em we got a stiff for pickup.

(Phone dialing)

EFFIE
Coroner's office? This is Effie in Dick Shamus's office. We got a stiff here for pickup. Got a knife in his back. Hold on. Boss...

SHAMUS
Yeah?

EFFIE
They said the earliest they could be here was tomorrow between twelve and four.

SHAMUS
In that case, when they get here, have 'em fix my cable. In the meantime, let's prop him up in the waiting room. If anyone comes in they'll just think he's a client.

EFFIE
With a knife in his back?

SHAMUS
Especially with a knife in his back.

(Music transition)

SHAMUS
It was time for another chat with Lisa Condo.

LISA
You didn't have to send the gendarmes, Shamus. You know me, a dinner and a movie and I would have told you everything.

SHAMUS

Everything?

LISA

Well, most everything.

SHAMUS

Don't get cute.

LISA

I can't help it. I'm adorable.

SHAMUS

Tell me what you know about a slug named Vinny "The Mug."

LISA

Never heard of him.

SHAMUS

Then tell me what you know about a mug named Vinny "The Slug."

LISA

Doesn't ring a bell.

SHAMUS

Okay. What about a slug named Vinny "The Bug?"

LISA

Are these gentlemen related, somehow?

SHAMUS

What makes you say that?

LISA

For one thing, they're all named Vinny.

SHAMUS

And they got one other name in common.

LISA

What's that?

SHAMUS

Ursulala. You're very ugly stepdaughter.

LISA

I admit Ursulala wasn't going to be crowned Miss Universe, but there's no reason to be cruel.

SHAMUS

Whatever you want to call him, Ursulala just bought the farm.

LISA
I'm surprised.

SHAMUS
Why's that?

LISA
He never expressed an interest in animal husbandry.

SHAMUS
Bought the farm as in pushing up daisies, achieving room temperature, checked into the wooden Waldorf, on a permanent vacation, rang down the curtain, no longer eligible for the census.

LISA
You mean he's dead?

SHAMUS
You could say that. It just wouldn't be as colorful.

LISA
How'd he die?

SHAMUS
The knife in his back may have had something to do with it.

LISA
How did a knife get in his back?

SHAMUS
We think somebody may have put it there.

LISA
Who?

SHAMUS
I thought you could tell us.

LISA
Me? Why me?

SHAMUS
When a mug like Vinny goes around in a dress pretending to be somebody's stepdaughter, it raises suspicions.

LISA
You don't think I killed Hobart.

SHAMUS
Is that what you called him?

LISA
He told me his name was Hobart J. Percywhistle

SHAMUS
Did you bump him off?

LISA
Why would I want to kill Hobart? He was teaching me to cha cha.

SHAMUS
Maybe he knew too much about your operation. Maybe he wanted in on the action. Maybe you didn't want to let him in on the action. Maybe he pushed a little too hard to get in on the action. Maybe you pushed back just as hard to keep him from getting in on the action. Maybe he pushed back even harder to get back in on the action. Maybe you pushed back even...

(Sound of a face beingslapped)

SHAMUS
Hey, you slugged me. What was that all about?

LISA
You were being ambivalent.

SHAMUS
Maybe I was and maybe I wasn't.

LISA
Don't make me slug you again.

SHAMUS
Keep stallin' dimple hips and I might have to get rough.

LISA
Promises. Promises.

SHAMUS
Come on. Spill or I'll have to book you on a 902.

LISA
Does that come with dinner and a movie?

SHAMUS
I know all about you and the Cinderella girl. About how you used her to get to Prince Charming.

LISA
I don't know any Cinderella girl.

SHAMUS
She knows you. Say you're her wicked stepmother. Says you set up the scam to sink your hooks into Prince Whatshisname. So, why don't you make it easy on yourself. Tell me what you know.

LISA
All I know is a couple of months ago, some guy came to see me.

SHAMUS
What guy?

LISA
Never told me his name

SHAMUS
And you didn't ask.

LISA
The pouch full of gold coins said all I needed to know.

SHAMUS
What was the cabbage for?

LISA
Rent. For an apartment for his girlfriend.

SHAMUS
What did this mysterious renter look like?

LISA
Mousy.

SHAMUS
The girl?

LISA
No, she was young, sweet, innocent with shoulders carved from the finest alabaster, a smile as fresh as a morning sunrise and a body like a brick pagoda.

SHAMUS
Did she have a name?

LISA
Everybody's got a name.

SHAMUS
Some people more than one. What was hers?

LISA
Never said.

SHAMUS
So you rented an apartment to a girl with no name paid for by a guy with no name. What else?

LISA
I took her shoe shopping.

SHAMUS
Is this one of the shoes.

LISA
Looks like it.

SHAMUS
Where does Vinny fit in?

LISA
I told you I don't know any Vinny.

SHAMUS
Hobart then.

LISA
He said the guy who rented the apartment heard you'd be snooping around. The plan was for Hobart to pretend to be my stepdaughter so you'd think I'd bought the shoe for her... Him... Whatever.

SHAMUS
But the shoe didn't fit.

LISA
I didn't say it was a good plan.

EFFIE
Hey boss.

LISA
What is it?

EFFIE
There's something in the newspaper you oughta see.

LISA
Don't go anywhere, apricot ears. I'm still not buying your story. I'm sure we're gonna find your prints all over the knife they took out of Vinny.

EFFIE
They already identified the prints.

SHAMUS
I knew it.

EFFIE
They belonged to Vinny's wife. Seems she caught him doin' the horizontal mambo with a waitress from Burger King.

SHAMUS
Well, he was a dance instructor.

EFFIE
But if his wife was the one who checked him in to the Tombstone Towers, why would he stumble into your office?

SHAMUS
Maybe he wanted me to know he'd been shot.

EFFIE
Stabbed.

SHAMUS
Stabbed.

EFFIE
But why?

SHAMUS
I guess we'll never know.

EFFIE
This story in today's paper might help. Look at this picture.

SHAMUS
That's her. That's the dame. Only here it says her name is Sarah Bellum.

EFFIE
I ran a check on her. Seems she's got a list of aliases as long as.... well, let's say your arm. She's also known as Cara Van, Charity Case, Milly Gram, Polly Esther, Rose Bush and Sue Flay. She's wanted in six kingdoms for impersonating a damsel in distress.

SHAMUS
And according to this, in one hour she'll be taking on a another handle. Mrs. Prince Charming.

LISA
More likely, Princess Charming. That's the one I'd go with.

SHAMUS
Effie, my sweet, keep an eye on this one.

EFFIE
Where are you going?

SHAMUS

To stop a wedding.

LISA

He always was a romantic.

(Transitional wedding music)

MINISTER

Dearly beloved we are gathered here today to bring together in holy matrimony, Prince Alfonse William Robert Hastings Oxford Jonathan Milford Anthony Philip William … again… Albert Constantine Charming, Prince of Lyman on Twill, Hutchings on Vetch, Twicky on Guss and Jam on Toast and Miss Sarah Bellum. If the groom will repeat after me. I Alfonse William Robert Hastings Oxford Jonathan Milford Anthony Philip William … again… Albert Constantine Charming.

PRINCE

I, Alfonse William Robert Hastings Oxford Jonathan Milford Anthony Philip William … again… Albert Constantine Charming.

MINISTER

Take thee Sarah Bellum

PRINCE

Take thee Sara Bellum.

MINISTER

To be my lawfully wedded wife.

PRINCE

To be my lawfully wedded wife.

MINISTER

And now if the bride will please repeat after me. I Sarah Bellum.

CINDERELLA

I, Sarah Bellum

MINISTER

Take thee Prince Alfonse William Robert Hastings Oxford Jonathan Milford Anthony Philip William … again… Albert Constantine Charming.

CINDERELLA

Take thee Prince Alfonse William Robert Hastings Oxford Jonathan Milford Anthony Philip William … again… Albert Constantine Charming for everything I can for as long as I can.

SHAMUS
Stop! Stop!

PRINCE
Mr. Shamus, what do you think you're doing?

SHAMUS
You can't marry her Prince.

PRINCE
Yes, I can.

SHAMUS
No, you can't.

PRINCE
Yes, I can.

SHAMUS
No you can't.

PRINCE
(singing)
Yes, I can, yes I can, yes I can.

SHAMUS
She's a fraud.

PRINCE
A fraud?

SHAMUS
She's not who she says she is, whatever it was she told you she was.

CINDERELLA
(syrupy southern
belle accent)
Oh fiddly dee, Princey, don't you listen to a word he's saying. The man is obviously deranged.

SHAMUS
He name isn't even Sara Bellum.

CINDERELLA
It most certainly is. I come from a long line of Bellums. There's my mother Momma Bellum. My father Daddy Bellum. My mother's brother Uncle Bellum… And my Daddy's sister…
(pause)

EVERYBODY
Auntie Bellum.

SHAMUS
She told me her name was Katie Cinderella O'Hara. Depending on the time and place she also goes by Barb Dwyer, Claire Annette Reid and Lily Pond.

CINDERELLA
Oh, fiddly dee. Can't you see he just wants to break us up? I didn't want to tell you this, honeysuckle, because I know how jealous you are when other men look at me. But, well, he's in love with me. He told me so himself.

PRINCE
Why Mr. Shamus. I'm appalled. Chagrined and appalled... Chagrined, appalled and several other words that mean chagrined and appalled.

SHAMUS
If she's so poor and downtrodden like she says, where'd she get the dough ray me to pay for the gown, the jewels and the custom made shoes she wore to the ball?

CINDERELLA
There's a very simple explanation.

SHAMUS
Let's hear it.

CINDERELLA
Well... I have a fairy godmother.

PRINCE
There you see. She has a fairy godmother.

SHAMUS
You have a fairy godmother alright. And he's standing right next to you. Isn't that right, Looney?

LACKEY
Lackey... It's Lackey.

PRINCE
Why he looks nothing like a fairy godmother.. Fairy godmothers have wings and high, fluttery voices. Besides, he couldn't afford diamonds. I pay him peanuts. Literally, I pay him peanuts.

SHAMUS
Have you checked the petty cash lately? Ask yourself this Prince, how did Blanche Dubois here get into your party that night?

PRINCE
She was invited obviously.

SHAMUS
Really? She wasn't anyone who was anyone. She didn't even know anyone who was anyone. But she did know Lousy, here.

LACKEY
Lackey. It's Lackey.

CINDERELLA
He's making all this up.

SHAMUS
I have an eye witness who identified the kid's picture in the paper as the man who rented an apartment from her to stash his girlfriend, our little Miss Orange Blossom Special here.

PRINCE
I find this very hard to believe Mr. Shamus.

SHAMUS
Then believe this Prince. Looney here...

LACKEY
Lackey... It's Lackey.

SHAMUS
... also paid my informant to take said girlfriend shoe shopping.

PRINCE
I fail to see the relevance. Women go shoe shopping all the time. And I do mean all the time.

SHAMUS
But this was no ordinary shoe. This shoe would only fit one foot. Her foot. The foot that you would track down and marry.

PRINCE
Marry a foot, that's ridiculous.

SHAMUS
The owner of the foot who would drain the royal treasury dry and split the loot with Loony here.

LACKEY
Lackey. It's Lackey.

CINDERELLA
My, you have a very vivid imagination, sir.

PRINCE
If my little mint julep said it never happened Shamus, it never happened.

SHAMUS
Wake up Charming. Our little man here is the only one who had the means, method and motivation.

PRINCE
What motivation could he possibly have?

SHAMUS
How about hatred and revenge for starters.

PRINCE
Who could he hate that much? He doesn't have a life. I see to that.

SHAMUS
You Prince. He hates you.

PRINCE
Don't be ridiculous, Shamus. I'm Prince Charming. Everybody loves me.

SHAMUS
Okay, Prince. I didn't want to do it. But you're forcing me to do it.

PRINCE
Do what?

SHAMUS
Play my hole card.

PRINCE
Hole card? What on earth are you talking about?

SHAMUS
The kid here has to be the brains behind the whole operation because...

PRINCE
Yes? Because?

SHAMUS
Because he is the least significant character in the story, with the least amount of lines and the last one anyone would ever suspect.

PRINCE
(aghast)
Lackey!!!

Made in the USA
Columbia, SC
08 May 2025